This book is dedicated to the One who opened my eyes to good nutrition. "Or do you know that your body is a temple of the Holy Spirit . . . for you have been bought with a price: therefore glorify God in your body."

I Corinthians 6:19-20, ASV

Recipes indicated with
an asterisk (*) can be
found in the index.

TABLE OF CONTENTS

I am grateful to my husband, Bill, for his support and patience during this project, and for encouraging me to share the experiences surrounding our current philosophy of nutrition.

Special thanks are due my "research assistants"—Jennifer, 4, and Jeremy, 2. They personally concocted all of the recipes in the *Kid's Corner* (with guidance from me, of course), helped with most of the other recipes, and tasted everything. A response of "Cookbook, Mommy!" was the criteria met by these recipes.

A respected family practice physician, Dr. Mahlon Maris, whose education, sensitivity and experience I value highly, gave me gentle guidance on controversial medical points, for which I am extremely grateful.

I am also indebted to my bi-weekly taste team—Barbara, Bev and Carol. Other regular tasters include Claudia, Donna, Edith, Kathy, Kaye and Sherry.

Without the clerical help of Carol and Sherry, I could not have succeeded in getting this book into manuscript form; and without the business knowledge and enthusiasm of my good friend Jan, it would not be widely distributed. I am also grateful for my proofreaders—Pat West and Pat Wheeler.

I appreciate the co-operation of WATE-TV in Knoxville for releasing recipes from the *Starr Cookbook*. I was delighted with the willingness of *Good Housekeeping* and *Family Circle* magazines to share their recipes for my publication. Each magazine generously granted permission for two recipes.

Finally, I am indebted to the Quaker Oats Company for their generous sharing of creative ideas with oats.

PREFACE

I have been trying for a good while now to get people to change their diets by eliminating sugar and white flour, and by avoiding processed and artificially flavored foods. It all seems too simple and logical. The people to whom I speak over the television, radio, in journals and newspaper articles nod and agree. However, only about 5-10% of those exposed to my credible, scientific persuasions will even make an effort—like putting three instead of four teaspoons of sugar in their 15 daily cups of coffee.

Didn't they want to have fewer cavities, less fatigue, less sickness, increased cheerfulness? Sure, but dropping all their comfort foods and trying to graze in raw foods is too sudden and too much for most people who are hooked on certain tasty goodies. Gradualism may be the most successful option.

Mary Ann Pickard has taken healthy food out of the "nut" class and given it dignity, respectability and more—good taste. A nourishing food cannot nourish unless it is swallowed. Adults and children will love these foods, for which she has simple, easy recipes.

I am generally against the use of fructose and honey because they tend to promote the idea that food has to taste sweet. So use these natural sweeteners sparingly as Mary Ann does, for a few months while you are getting your family weaned away from sugar. Then finally announce that the bees gave up! Everyone will know you are teasing, but maybe you've changed your family members' tastes and life-styles enough that they can handle the absence of that sweet-sweet sugary taste.

Now I know why I could not get the world to change its habits: I did not have *"Feasting Naturally"* to implement my logic.

FOREWORD

Bon appetit!
Lendon H. Smith, M.D.
Portland, Oregon

Our home has been completely free of refined sugars, flours and grains for a full two years now. As I look back on the beginning, it is clear to me that nothing short of a miracle brought this to pass!

God blessed me with a very powerful husband, solid in his beliefs and secure in his masculinity. He is the final authority on everything in our home and the human source of my security as a wife and mother. For this, I am continually thankful. However, my husband, Bill, has a stubborn streak in him you would not believe; I guess it goes along with the strength of his personality. For this, I admit, I am not continually thankful!

Slightly more than two years ago, our little world was in a pretty shaky condition. Financial pressures, business tensions, and blatant disregard for his physical health had plunged Bill into a sorry state. He was 50 pounds overweight, sedentary, tense, and suffering from acute chest pains and high blood pressure...at 30 years of age.. In short, he functioned ineffectively as a husband and a father.

I mentioned the stubborn streak...it was precisely what kept me from getting through to him with any of my "help". When the chest pains started, I really became scared. I was expecting our second child at the time, and was not at all anxious to become a rich widow. So, I finally turned the whole problem over to God, which was what I should have done in the first place.

In two weeks, Bill was on the original "Weight Watchers" diet, one of the best balanced dietary programs around. That was nice, but not particularly miraculous. What was amazing was that he stayed on it with no help from me! (Understand that Bill was not your average "weekend dessert lover". He's been known to keep a box of sugar cubes in his desk for snacking or to eat an entire can of frosting at one sitting!)

Thirty pounds after the diet began, Bill ordered a copy of *Psychodietetics* by Cheraskin and Ringsdorf. After reading it, he decided to eliminate refined sugars, flours and grains from his diet. An additional twenty pound loss followed, then I was convinced. The physical, emotional and mental changes I saw in him, the ability to handle stress without overreacting, the

BEFORE YOU BEGIN ...

-3-

significant decrease in blood pressure, the markedly improved self image, all were effects of a simple change in diet!

I soon realized that this diet could have a positive impact on our children: imagine the possibility of raising children from preschool age who would never experience the harmful effects of sugar dependency! Both Bill and I began to study nutrition, reading everything about it we could find. I don't present myself as an expert in the field of nutrition. I haven't conducted any scientific experiments aside from those on our own family. However, the studies of others have certainly opened my eyes to some significant facts.

We found no documented research stating sugar to be beneficial for the body's use. The extreme philosophy to which we adhere is supported by the thorough research of numerous biochemists and physicians. The very basis of this research is the fact that the cerebral cortex, from which all conscious bodily activity initiates, requires a steady flow of glucose in order to function properly. The brain comprises 2% of the body's weight, yet requires 25% of its nutrients. An imbalance of blood sugar can cause the cortex to initiate inappropriate, even bizarre responses to stimuli. So, you can see why "We must protect the cerebral cortex." (Dr. Lendon Smith in *Improving Your Child's Behavior Chemistry.*)

All foods can be eventually converted into glucose, which supplies energy for the body's use. The steady flow of glucose, which the cortex demands, is achieved by the ingestion of complex foods which give a gradual breakdown to glucose, along with the mediating effect of insulin. The result is a steady, even flow of glucose or blood sugar to the entire body.

Conversely, an intake of refined sugar causes a sudden rise in blood sugar level.

Situation: An individual with a steady blood level of glucose.

Insertion: one candy bar or cola for "instant energy"

Result: a surge of energy; a "high"; a sudden rise in blood glucose level triggering an enormous output of insulin to the entire body in an effort to regulate the blood sugar.

Inevitability: a "low", a state of depression, and a craving for more sugar or another high, usually a few hours after the "energy snack".

Solution: eat more sugar????

Did you ever wonder why a famous soft drink was recommended for consumption at "10, 2 & 4"? Given a sugar-laced breakfast and lunch, those time slots occur every 2 hours at the lows which inevitably will follow the highs. This is the infamous roller-coaster syndrome that has, by some estimates, up to half the American population in its grip.

These periodic lows are actually episodes of functional hypoglycemia, or low blood sugar. It has been called the most undiagnosed disease existing today. Countless people are walking around less than healthy, experiencing vague symptoms that are often lumped into the psychosomatic mold.

These symptoms may include several of the following:
    dizziness

* headaches, fatigue or exhaustion
  fainting or blackouts
* narcolepsy (abnormal attacks of sleepiness)
* muscle pains and cramps
  numbness
* insomnia
  nightmares
* irritability
  crying spells
  restlessness
  nervous breakdown
* inability to concentrate
  excessive worry and anxiety
  depression
* forgetfulness
  illogical fears
  suicidal thoughts
  tremors
  cold sweats
  inner trembling
  uncoordination
  convulsion
  fast and/or noticeable heart beat
  blurred vision
* allergies
  itching and/or crawling sensations
  neurodermatitis
  arthritic pains
  loss of sexual drive
  impotency
  shortness of breath

(Source: *Psychodietetics*, Cheraskin and Ringsdorf)

True hypoglycemia can be diagnosed by your doctor. The trouble, however, is that when your symptoms don't point to anything else, physicians often tell you the problem is "between your ears." Since "It can masquerade as a hundred physical diseases—from epilepsy to gastric ulcers—and embellish the symptoms with a perfect simulation of neurosis or psychosis, it is often difficult to pinpoint." (Carlton Fredericks, *Low Blood Sugar And You*). After years of psychosomatic guilt, it really will be in your head, when perhaps the solution is as simple as a dietary adjustment.

If you suspect you are suffering from low blood sugar, see your physician. He can diagnose true hypoglycemia with a 6 hour glucose tolerance test. Both functional and true hypoglycemia can be controlled by eliminating refined sugars from your diet.

The most frightening thing about the injustice we do to our bodies by eating so much refined carbohydrate is that it leads to hypoglycemia, and that is a precursor to diabetes. In simple language, the pancreas overreacts

-5-

to the sugar surge so much that it eventually will not react at all, which is the problem in diabetes. Since the number of diabetics in our country is doubling each year, this is a significant reason for you to consider a dietary change.

Therefore, the rollercoaster syndrome is a major reason for avoiding refined sugars. Carlton Fredericks states in *Low Blood Sugar And You* that "For one person in every ten, sugar is a deadly food... for that person, a little sugar is akin to a little carbolic acid."

"If only a small fraction of what is already known about the effects of sugar were to be revealed in relation to any other material used as a food additive, that material would promptly be banned." (John Yudkin, *Sweet and Dangerous*). If you think that statement represents a viewpoint too extreme for you, consider the mounting evidence which links excess sugar consumption to the following organic diseases:

  alcoholism
  schizophrenia
  manic depressive syndrome
  allergies
  senility
  juvenile hyperactivity
  obesity
  arthritis
  premature aging
  adolescent bed wetting
  cardiovascular accidents
  gastric distress and ulcers
  cancer
  skin disorders
  visual problems

(See reading list for research).

There is still more evidence against refined sugars. An increased intake of refined sugars raises blood levels of serum lipids, which can be implicated in coronary disease. Therefore, one way to control your risk of coronary disease is to greatly reduce or eliminate the amount of refined carbohydrate in your diet. However, the indiscriminate consumption of animal fats and other hydrogenated substances should be avoided, since it is also an important factor in heart disease.

Refined sugar is also infamous for a depletion of B vitamins, since they are essential to its metabolism. White sugar has no food value, and its position as a "quick energy" food has already been questioned. In addition, sugar creates a craving for more sugar, and therefore replaces the good foods your body so desperately needs. And, it is every bit as addictive as drugs, alcohol or cigarettes! If you don't agree, try giving up your sugar and find out.

Finally, sugar is widely accepted as being detrimental to dental health. Increased sugar consumption is the major factor in the dramatic increase of dental caries. (Realize, however, that dried fruits, peanut butter or raisins can do as much harm as sugar if teeth are not properly maintained.)

One interesting thing I've learned since studying nutrition is that if man would eat a more natural, unrefined diet, he would receive the total package of nutrients God intended for him when He put it all together. Case in point: white bread, the "staff of life"???

Around the turn of the century when our nation became more industrialized, people began to rely more on grocery stores than their own supply of food stuffs. Transportation of goods became necessary, and a longer shelf life was essential for foods. Refined "enriched" flour was one answer to the problem, since the oil in the wheat germ made the flour more perishable. The bleaching and refining process removes all the nutrients from the flour, and the enrichment process is a mere token. The germ is the most essential part of the wheat; in it is a wealth of B vitamins, protein, vitamin E, and lecithin. And the bran contains the necessary bulk which promotes regularity and intestinal health. On top of that, highly refined flours and grains are quickly converted into glucose. Too much will cause the same effects as sugar. The same case can be made for polished rice; hence the emphasis in this book is on whole, unrefined, unprocessed foods—the way God gave them.

You are probably already familiar with the research done by Dr. Ben Feingold on hyperactivity in children as it relates to diet, particularly to refined sugars and artificial flavorings and colorings. In short, the child's brain cannot deal with the highs and lows of the rollercoaster syndrome when the sugar is eaten; therefore, he responds the only way he can—physically and very often erratically. Dr. Lendon Smith says that "The pediatrician should insist that all his patients nibble on protein; sugar should not be in any home...he should walk into school and ax down the candy machines and get protein snacks in all the classrooms."

Dr. Smith is right—I've taught in schools from ghetto to upper class and seen the behavior dysfunction when my children came in at 8:00 munching on a candy bar or doughnut and sipping a cola. And sending them off with a sugary breakfast cereal, white toast and jelly and a pre-sweetened vitamin C drink, is no better! No wonder the discipline situation in our schools is such a nightmare!

I'll admit that breakfast can be boring; who wants a poached egg and grapefruit every day? But it is so important for everyone, especially children, whose brains require twice as many nutrients as adults' brains, to start off the day with a balanced, protein rich breakfast. For this reason, I've included a special section for suggested breakfast menus. I hope it is beneficial to you.

Further study caused us to look at a total picture of health involving good nutrition, plenty of sunshine, aerobic exercise, and vitamin supplements. I won't go into that here, except to say that unless our food is totally homegrown and impeccably prepared, it is not likely we could obtain an adequate supply of vitamins from it. Vitamin research is a fascinating field; refer to the reading list for information on leading biochemists, nutritionists and physicians who have made significant contributions in this field.

We really are a normal family. We don't have antennae or three heads; we simply eat a more natural, unrefined diet. Countless people who noticed the dramatic change in Bill commented to us that they'd do the same thing if they knew how to cook without refined sugars. Because of this need and the frustration of watching a close friend suffer from the effects of a lifetime of excess sugar consumption, the idea came to me for *Feasting Naturally.* Writing it has been a family project, and one we have all enjoyed a great deal.

Basically, we follow the "Optimal Diet" as defined by Cheraskin and Ringsdorf in *Psychodietetics.* We've learned to be good stewards of our bodies by eating these foods:

Fruits, fruit juices and vegetables
Eggs, cheese and milk
Meat, fish and poultry
Whole grain breads and cereals.
Nuts, seeds and 100% peanut butter

We studiously avoid these foods:

Hidden and refined sugars
Artificially processed foods
Foods containing white sugar, brown sugar, confectioners sugar, turbinado sugar, raw or natural sugar and sweeteners, white noodles, nitrates, and other chemical additives

There is nothing at all wrong with eating plain, simple foods: fruit and cheese, steak and baked potato, green salads, broiled chicken and steamed vegetables. Neither is there anything wrong with eating the foods made from recipes in this book. Either way, exclusively, would soon become dull. A mixture of these recipes coupled with a balance of the basic foods is what we enjoy. Desserts will become less important to you; we eat them only on occasion. When sweeteners are needed, we use raw honey and fructose.

Fructose, or fruit sugar, is the sugar found in honey. Also available in powdered or liquid form, it is preferable over other sugars because it requires very little insulin to be metabolized. Therefore, it maintains the necessary steady flow of blood sugar to the body, without starting the rollercoaster. Also, since it doesn't excite your blood sugar level, you're not hungry two hours after eating a food sweetened with fructose.

Fructose is sweeter than sucrose or refined sugar. In addition, it contains the same calories, gram for gram, as sugar, but since you use 1/2 - 1/3 less, the caloric content is proportionately less. One strange property of fructose is that it sweetens cold liquids better than hot ones—hot liquids require more fructose to achieve an equal sweetening. Fructose is a true energy food, however; overuse of any concentrated carbohydrate can be detrimental to the body's function. Be careful not to substitute fructose for sucrose and continue your craving for sweets; rather, try to lessen that sweet tooth in favor of more complex foods.

If you cheat and substitute refined sugar or refined flour in the dessert recipes, you will be sadly disappointed! The physical properties of honey, texture differences of wholegrains, water absorption of fructose, and variations in yield are all factors that were adjusted for these recipes.

Some foods are specifically recommended in recipes for their particular nutritional bonuses; for example:

Safflower oil—contains essential fatty acids

Stone ground flours and meals—because they are the least processed flours

Yogurt—contains active bacterial cultures which aid in digestion

Unfortunately, eating this way does cost a bit more. However, when you eliminate the junk and prepared foods from your grocery list, you'll only notice a slight rise in expense. You can cut your cost by following these suggestions:

1. Buy seeds in large (5 lb.) packages, toast them yourself and snack on them. Substitute for nuts when possible.
2. Freeze or dry vegetables and fruits in season, preferably from your own garden.
3. Buy wholegrain flours in bulk and store them in the freezer to use as needed.
4. Shell your own nuts in season, especially roasted peanuts and store in the freezer.
5. Substitute tuna for the more expensive seafoods such as shrimp or crab.
6. Buy raw honey in bulk.
7. Buy meat in bulk and freeze.
8. Re-use juices for pickle recipes up to 5 times.
9. Watch for specials and stock up on staples.
10. Buy powdered eggs and use them in baking.
11. Shop around for the best fructose price: I have seen it as high as $14.95 for 10 oz. and as low as $3.49 for 2 lbs.
12. Save stock from meats and poultry for soups.
13. Make your own breads.

Making your own bread is economical, healthful and fun! However, it is not mandatory. If you read labels carefully, you can find 100% whole wheat breads without sugar or preservatives. You can also take advantage of other supermarket choices besides fresh fruits, juices and vegetables, meats and dairy products. By carefully reading labels, you will find other things you can buy, just beware of clever labelling. Keep in mind that fresh or frozen is always better than canned, because of greater vitamin retention. On a typical shopping day, my grocery bill is composed of 75% fresh fruits and vegetables, milk and juice, and 25% meats, cheeses, paper products and miscellaneous items.

In order to use the recipes in this book, you'll just need the usual kitchen tools—blender, mixer, food grinder. A microwave is nice, but not essential. Do invest in a vegetable steamer to fit in your pots; they make vegetable preparation and taste much more enjoyable and nutritious. You can get one easily for under $5. A nice tool to acquire is a mixer with dough hook or a food processor that will handle yeast dough. Either will enable you to make any yeast dough easily.

I know my children are going to eat sugar, sometimes by accident and sometimes on purpose. That I concede; I can't worry about every morsel they eat away from home. With the sugar industry thrusting a large portion of its ad money at children, who don't know any better, I feel I must fight back with sound nutritional training. I can give them a strong foundation and present them with the good foods, training their taste buds while they are still young. And isn't that my responsibility as a parent—the mental, emotional, physical, spiritual and nutritional training of my children so that they can function at their full capabilities and meet life with security and confidence? I'm convinced that it is!

Note: *As with any dietary program, consult your doctor before beginning anything this book advocates, especially if you are a diabetic requiring insulin.*

SUGGESTED READING LIST

1. *Aerobics for Women*—Kenneth and Mildred Cooper

2. *Feed Your Kids Right*—Lendon H. Smith, M.D.

3. *Improving Your Child's Behavior Chemistry*—Lendon H. Smith, M.D.

4. *Low Blood Sugar and You*—Carlton Fredericks, Ph.D.

5. *Meganutrients For Your Nerves*—H.L. Newbold, M.D.

6. *Nutrition Against Disease*—Roger J. Williams, Ph.D.

7. *Psychodietetics*—Emanuel Cheraskin, M.D., D.M.D. and W.M. Ringsdorf, D.M.D., M.S.

8. *Supermarket Handbook*—Nikki and David Goldbeck

9. *Supernutrition*—Richard A. Passwater, Ph.D.

10. *Sweet and Dangerous*—John Yudkin, M.D.

11. *The Aerobics Way*—Kenneth H. Cooper, M.D.

12. *Why Your Child is Hyperactive*—Ben F. Feingold, M.D.

BREADS

CREAMY PANCAKES
"light and delicious"

4 eggs
1 1/2 c. plain yogurt
1/2 c. milk
1/2 c. unbleached flour

1/2 c. wheat germ
1/4 c. oats
1 tsp. soda
1 tsp. salt

Combine dry ingredients; mix eggs, yogurt and milk together and add to dry ingredients all at once. Stir until moistened; pour 1/4 cup of batter into greased griddle. Cook until bubbly and dry-looking, then turn and brown on other side.

Preparation time: 30 minutes   Yield: 12 (3 inch) pancakes

APPLE PANCAKES

1/2 c. raisins
2 beaten eggs
1 1/3 c. milk
1 c. whole wheat flour
1/2 c. unprocessed bran

1 tsp. salt
3 Tbsp. honey
1 Tbsp. cinnamon
1 Tbsp. baking powder
2 tart apples, peeled and shredded

Combine dry ingredients; add eggs, milk and honey all at once, stirring until moistened. Add apples and raisins; mix thoroughly by hand. Using about 1/4 cup batter per pancake, spoon onto hot buttered griddle, spreading out to 3 inch rounds. Cook until bubbly, turn, and cook until golden brown.

Preparation time: 30 minutes   Yield: 15 (3 inch) pancakes

BLUEBERRY BRANCAKES   *1-20-90*

2 c. whole wheat flour
1 c. unprocessed bran
1/2 c. chopped nuts
1 Tbsp. baking powder
1 tsp. salt
1 tsp. cinnamon

2 c. milk
2 eggs
1/2 c. honey
1/4 c. safflower oil
1/2 c. fresh or unthawed, frozen
   blueberries

Mix dry ingredients together; combine milk, eggs, honey and oil and stir into dry mixture. Allow to stand for 2 or 3 minutes, then add blueberries and stir to mix. Drop about 1/4 cup batter onto preheated griddle until golden brown on both sides. Serve right away.

Preparation time: 20 minutes   Yield: 12 brancakes

BREAKFAST CRUNCHIES
"tasty delicate cookies"

2/3 c. butter or margarine
2/3 c. honey
1 egg
1 tsp. vanilla
3/4 c. unbleached or
   whole wheat flour

1/2 tsp. soda
1/2 tsp. salt
1 1/2 c. uncooked oats
1 c. shredded Cheddar cheese
1/2 c. wheat germ
1/2 c. browned sausage, drained

Cream butter, honey, egg and vanilla until smooth; add flour, soda and salt. Stir in oats, cheese, wheat germ and sausage and drop by teaspoonfuls onto greased cookie sheets. Bake at 350 degrees for 12-15 minutes; cool for a minute, then turn onto racks to finish cooling.

Preparation time: 25 minutes   Yield: 3 dozen

WHOLE WHEAT LUNCHEON PUFFS

1 c. water
1/2 c. butter or margarine
2-3 dashes Tabasco sauce

1 c. whole wheat flour
1/2 tsp. salt
4 eggs, room temperature

Bring water, butter and Tabasco sauce to a boil. Add flour and salt all at once, stirring with wire whisk. Add eggs, one at a time, stirring vigorously. Cook and stir over medium heat for 1 minute, or until mixture leaves the sides of the pan. Drop by rounded tablespoonfuls onto greased cookie sheets. Bake at 400 degrees for 40-45 minutes, cool completely; freeze or use. Just before serving, split and fill with a favorite meat or fish salad.

Preparation time: 55 minutes   Yield: 12 puffs

BUTTERMILK WHOLE-WHEAT BISCUITS

1 c. unbleached flour
1 c. whole wheat flour
2 tsp. baking powder
1/2 tsp. salt

1/4 tsp. soda
1/4 c. melted butter
2/3 c. buttermilk

Combine dry ingredients and stir in butter, blending until mixture reaches a crumb-like texture. Add buttermilk stirring until mixture forms a ball. Handling as little as possible, knead lightly, then pat to 3/4 inch thickness. Cut with floured cutter and bake at 425 degrees for 10-15 minutes. These will not be a light, fluffy biscuit, but the flavor is good.

Preparation time: 20 minutes   Yield: 6-8 biscuits

WHOLE WHEAT RUSKS
"Crisp toast-like biscuits to pour creamed meats or poached egg dishes over"

1 pkg. dry yeast
2 1/4 c. whole wheat flour
1/2 c. unbleached flour
3 Tbsp. honey

3/4 tsp. salt
4 Tbsp. butter or margarine
1 1/4 c. milk

Place yeast, whole wheat flour and 1/2 cup unbleached flour in mixing bowl. Combine, honey, salt, butter and milk in a saucepan and heat until liquids are very warm. Add to flour mixture and beat on medium speed of mixer until well mixed. If batter seems sticky, add 1/4-1/2 cup more unbleached flour. Continue beating for 3-5 minutes, until dough holds together in a ball. Cover and let rise 1 hour, until doubled.

Punch dough down; shape into about 20 (3 inch) oval rolls. Place on greased cookie sheet and cover. Let rise 45 minutes - 1 hour. Bake at 400 degrees for 15 minutes, split and bake for 5-7 more minutes, until toasted. Remove from oven, cool, and return to oven to dry overnight.

Preparation time: overnight   Yield: 40 Rusks

PERFECT BISCUITS

2 c. unbleached flour
1/2 tsp. salt
4 tsp. baking powder
1/2 tsp. cream of tartar

2 tsp. honey
1 stick butter
2/3 c. milk

Sift dry ingredients together, cut in shortening. Mix milk and honey, add to other ingredients and knead lightly. Roll or pat to 3/4 inch thickness and cut. Place on a greased baking sheet and bake for 10-15 minutes at 450 degrees.

Preparation time: 20-25 minutes   Yield: 8 (2 1/2 inch) biscuits

EXTRA-LIGHT BISCUITS

2 c. unbleached flour
1 Tbsp. baking powder
1/4 tsp. soda
1 tsp. salt

1 tsp. honey
1 c. yogurt (plain)
1/4 c. butter, room temperature

In a large bowl, mix dry ingredients with a pastry blender. Cut in the butter until the mixture resembles coarse crumbs. Then add honey and yogurt, stirring with a fork. Knead lightly with hands, adding a little water if needed. Pat to 3/4 inch thickness, and cut with small biscuit cutter. Place on ungreased cookie sheet and bake at 425 degrees for 10-15 minutes.

This recipe can also be successfully doubled or tripled, with extra biscuits being frozen before baking. When ready to cook, remove as many as needed and bake 20-25 minutes at 425 degrees. Keeps 1 month.

Preparation time: 30 minutes   Yield: 12-14 biscuits

LUNCHTIME BISCUIT FOLDOVERS

2 c. unbleached flour
1 Tbsp. baking powder
1 tsp. salt
1 stick butter or margarine

3/4 c. milk
2 c. chicken or steak salad,
    Cheddar cheese, or other
    favorite filling

Stir together flour, baking powder and salt. Cut in butter with pastry blender until mixture is the consistency of coarse crumbs. Add milk and stir with fork. Flour hands and squeeze dough until all is moistened and dough forms a ball.

Turn out onto floured surface and roll or pat out until dough is 1/2 inch thick. Cut with 2 1/2 inch round cookie cutter and flatten each ball' out to a 4 or 5 inch circle. Place 2 tablespoonfuls of filling in the center, fold over to a half-moon shape, and seal edges with a fork. Place on a greased cookie sheet and bake at 400 degrees for 15-18 minutes.

Preparation time: 40 minutes   Yield: 10-12 biscuits

CHEESE BALLS

1 1/2 c. sharp Cheddar cheese,
  grated
1 scant c. of unbleached flour

1/2 tsp. salt
1/4 tsp. cayenne
1 stick butter

Cream cheese and butter together, stir in dry ingredients and knead lightly until dough forms a ball. Form into balls, and bake at 400 degrees for 10-12 minutes. Serve piping hot or cool and store in tightly covered container.

Preparation time: 25 minutes   Yield: 3 - 3 1/2 dozen

WHOLE-WHEAT ENGLISH MUFFINS

1 c. milk
2 Tbsp. honey
1 tsp. salt
3 Tbsp. butter

1 envelope dry yeast
1 1/2 c. whole wheat flour
3 1/2 c. unbleached flour

Scald milk, stirring in honey, salt and butter. Cool to lukewarm. Measure 1 cup warm water into bowl and dissolve yeast into that. Add milk mixture to water and yeast, then stir in whole wheat flour and 1 1/2 cups unbleached flour. Beat on low speed of mixer until a soft dough forms. Add enough remaining flour to make a stiff dough, then knead on a floured surface for 2-3 minutes. Put into greased bowl, turning to grease top. Cover and let rise until double, about 1 hour. Punch down; divide into halves. Pat to 1/2 inch thickness and cut out 3 inch rounds with floured cutter. Let rise on ungreased cookie sheets until double, then bake on medium hot greased griddle until well-browned on each side, about 5 minutes per side. Cool on racks; split, toast, and serve.

Preparation time: 2 hours 45 minutes   Yield: 18

WHOLE-WHEAT CORN MUFFINS

1 c. whole wheat flour	1 1/3 c. milk
1 c. stone ground yellow	1/4 c. honey
corn meal	1/4 c. safflower oil
4 tsp. baking powder	1/4 c. onions, chopped fine
1/2 tsp. salt	1/4 c. roasted sunflower seeds
2 beaten eggs	

Stir together the dry ingredients except sunflower seeds. Mix the eggs, milk, honey and oil together, then add to the other mixture. Stir just until moistened, then spoon the thin batter into paper-lined muffin pans, filling 2/3 full. Sprinkle each muffin with sunflower seeds and bake for about 20 minutes in a 400 degree oven.

Preparation time: 30 minutes   Yield: 18 muffins

CORNBREAD

3 c. stone ground yellow	3 eggs
corn meal	1/2 c. safflower oil
2 tsp. baking powder	1 1/2 c. corn
1/2 tsp. soda	1 c. chopped onion
1/2 tsp. salt	8 chopped Jalapeno peppers
1 1/2 c. milk	1 1/2 c. sharp, grated Cheddar
1/2 c. plain yogurt	cheese

In a large bowl, mix dry ingredients together. Add milk, oil, eggs and yogurt; stir until moistened. Add remaining ingredients; mix well. Pour into greased 9x 13 inch baking pan and bake at 350 degrees for 25-30 minutes or until done.

Preparation time: 45 minutes   Yield: 24 squares

BLUEBERRY BARLEY MUFFINS

1 1/2 c. whole wheat flour
1 c. barley flour
1 1/2 tsp. baking powder
3/4 tsp. salt
1 tsp. cloves
1/2 tsp. soda
1 2/3 c. buttermilk

1/2 c. honey
2 beaten eggs
1/4 c. safflower oil
1 Tbsp. cinnamon
3 Tbsp. fructose
1/2 c. blueberries

Combine dry ingredients: flours, baking powder, salt, cloves, and soda. Add honey, eggs and oil to buttermilk, and stir at once into dry ingredients, mixing by hand until moistened. Add blueberries to batter and fill greased or paper-lined muffin cups 2/3 full. Sprinkle with cinnamon and fructose mixture and bake at 400 degrees for 20-25 minutes.

Preparation time: 30 minutes   Yield: 12 muffins

ZUCCHINI MUFFINS

2 c. unbleached flour
3/4 c. wheat germ
1 Tbsp. baking powder
1 tsp. allspice
1 tsp. cinnamon

1 c. unpeeled, shredded zucchini
1/2 c. honey
3/4 c. + 2 Tbsp. evaporated milk
1/4 c. safflower oil
1 beaten egg

Stir together flour, wheat germ, baking powder and spices. Add zucchini. Combine milk, honey, oil and egg and add to first mixture. Stir only until dry ingredients are moistened (batter will be thick). Spoon into greased or paper-lined muffin cups. Bake at 375 degrees for 20-25 minutes.

Preparation time: 30 minutes   Yield: 12 muffins

PEANUT BUTTER AND HONEY MUFFINS

2 c. whole wheat flour
1 c. chopped, salted peanuts
1 Tbsp. baking powder
1/4 tsp. salt

1 1/3 c. evaporated milk
3/4 c. honey
1 c. natural style peanut butter
1 egg

Stir dry ingredients together, then combine milk, honey, peanut butter and egg; add all at once to dry ingredients, stirring only to moisten. Fill paper-lined muffin cups 2/3 full and bake at 350 degrees for 20-25 minutes.

Preparation time: 35 minutes   Yield: 18 muffins

BRAN MUFFINS

3 c. unprocessed bran
1 c. boiling water
1 c. honey
2 1/4 c. unbleached flour
2 1/2 tsp. soda

1 tsp. salt
1 stick butter or margarine
2 c. buttermilk
2 eggs

Combine 1 cup bran and the boiling water; stir well and allow to stand for 5 minutes. Meanwhile, cream butter or margarine and add honey slowly, beating until creamy. Beat in eggs, then add remaining ingredients. Stir until well-mixed, then beat for 1 minute. Pour into greased or paper-lined muffin cups filling 2/3 full and bake at 400 degrees for 20 or 25 minutes. Or, spoon batter into plastic container and cover tightly; refrigerate. Will keep in refrigerator 6 weeks; use as needed.

Preparation time: 10 minutes   Yield: 1 1/2 quart batter
Hint: Vary the muffins by adding dried fruits, nuts or raisins as desired.

PUMPKIN-RAISIN MUFFINS

2 eggs
1 c. honey
1 c. pumpkin (canned or mashed, cooked)
3/4 c. safflower oil
1 1/3 c. unbleached flour
Dash salt

1 tsp. baking powder
1 tsp. soda
1 tsp. cinnamon
1/2 tsp. allspice
1/2 c. raisins
1/2 c. chopped nuts

Beat eggs well; add honey, oil, and pumpkin. Add dry ingredients and mix well. Stir in raisins and nuts; fill paper-lined muffin cups 2/3 full. Bake at 350 degrees for 20 minutes.

Preparation time: 25 minutes   Yield: 18 muffins

TRICIA'S CHEESE MUFFINS

1 1/2 c. whole wheat flour
1/2 c. wheat germ
4 tsp. baking powder
1/2 tsp. salt
1 c. milk

1 egg
1 Tbsp. honey
3 Tbsp. softened butter
2 c. grated sharp cheese

Combine dry ingredients; stir in milk, egg and honey. Add softened butter and cheese and stir until moistened. Spoon into greased muffin cups and bake at 400 degrees for 20-25 minutes.

Preparation time: 30 minutes   Yield: 12 muffins

APRICOT BREAD

1 c. unbleached flour	1/2 c. chopped nuts
1/2 c. whole wheat flour	1 1/4 c. milk
2 tsp. baking powder	1 c. dried apricots
1/2 tsp. soda	2 eggs
1 tsp. salt	1/3 c. safflower oil
1 c. rolled oats	3/4 c. honey

Stir together first seven ingredients. Place milk, apricots and eggs in blender; whirl until apricots are chopped fine. Pour over dry ingredients, add oil and honey and mix until all particles have been moistened. Place in a well-greased loaf pan and bake 1 hour at 350 degrees.

Preparation time: 1 1/4 hour   Yield: 1 loaf

POPPYSEED BREAD

1 c. milk	1 Tbsp. poppyseed
1/4 c. honey	1 c. warm water
1 Tbsp. salt	2 pkg. yeast
1 1/2 Tbsp. butter	4 1/2 c. unbleached flour

Scald milk; stir in honey, butter and salt. Cool to lukewarm. Soften yeast in warm water, add cooled milk mixture and mix well. Add poppyseed and flour, stirring to mix; then beat 5 minutes (dough will be sticky). Cover and let rise until tripled, about 1 hour. Stir down and turn into 2 greased (1 pound) loaf pans. Bake at 375 degrees for 30 minutes or until done. Turn out onto wire racks and brush with butter.

Preparation time: 2 hours   Yield: 2 (1 pound) loaves

BANANA BREAD

1/2 stick butter	1/2 c. whole wheat flour
1 c. honey	1 tsp. soda
3 mashed, very ripe bananas	1/4 tsp. salt
2 well-beaten eggs	1 c. chopped nuts
1 1/2 c. unbleached flour	

Cream butter until light. Drizzle in honey while mixer is running; beat until creamy. Add bananas and eggs, then dry ingredients. Stir in nuts, then turn into well-greased and floured 9 X 5 inch loaf pan and bake at 325 degrees for 1 hour.

Preparation time: 1 hour 15 minutes Yield: 1 loaf

CRANBERRY BREAD

1 1/2 c. unbleached flour
1/2 c. whole wheat flour
1 c. honey
1 1/2 tsp. baking powder
1/2 tsp. soda
1 tsp. salt

1 c. fresh cranberries, coarsely
  chopped
1/4 c. butter
1 Tbsp. orange rind
1 egg
1 c. chopped nuts

Sift together dry ingredients; cut in shortening until mixture resembles coarse corn meal. Combine honey, egg and orange rind and pour into dry ingredients. Stir just to dampen, then carefully fold in nuts and berries. Turn into 9 X 5 inch loaf pan, well greased and floured; bake at 350 degrees for 1 hour.

Preparation time: 1 hour 15 minutes   Yield: 1 loaf

DILLY BREAD

1 pkg. yeast
1/4 c. warm water
1 c. creamed cottage cheese
2 Tbsp. honey
1 Tbsp. instant minced onion
1 Tbsp. softened butter

2 tsp. dill seed
1 tsp. salt
1/4 tsp. soda
1 egg, room temperature
2 1/2 c. unbleached flour

Dissolve yeast in warm water. Heat cottage cheese and honey to lukewarm, then add to yeast mixture with onion, butter, dill seed, salt, soda and egg. Add enough flour to make a stiff dough; cover and let rise until doubled, about 1 hour. Stir dough down; turn into well greased loaf pan. Cover and let rise until doubled; about 1 hour. Bake at 350 degrees for 45-50 minutes. When done, turn out onto wire rack and brush with butter; sprinkle with salt.

Preparation time: 3 hours   Yield: 1 loaf

BRAN ROLLS

3/4 c. unprocessed bran
1 1/2 tsp. salt
2 pkg. yeast
1 c. water

1/2 c. margarine, room temperature
1/3 c. honey
1 egg, room temperature
3 - 3 1/4 c. unbleached flour

Combine bran, salt and yeast in a large bowl. Heat water, honey and margarine until liquids are very warm, (margarine does not need to melt) and add to bran mixture. Stir to mix, then beat at medium speed 2 minutes. Add egg and 1 cup flour; beat for 1 minute on medium speed. Add enough flour to make a stiff dough, then knead until smooth (about 8 minutes). Place in a greased bowl, turning to grease top. Cover and let rise until doubled, about 1 hour. Punch dough down; divide in half. Form each half into about 12 balls, then place in 2 greased (8 inch) round pans. Cover and let rise until doubled, about 1 hour. Bake at 375 degrees for about 20 minutes.

Preparation time: 3 hours   Yield: 2 dozen

WHOLE WHEAT ROLLS
(light and delicious)

2 pkg. dry yeast
4 1/2 c. whole wheat flour
1 c. unbleached flour
1 1/2 tsp. salt

1/3 c. honey
1/2 c. butter or margarine
2 1/2 c. milk

Combine yeast, whole wheat flour, 1 cup unbleached flour, and salt in mixing bowl. Heat honey, butter and milk until liquids are very warm. Add gradually to flour mixture, then mix on medium speed for 2 minutes. Knead in 1/2 cup unbleached flour until dough forms a ball (5-7 minutes). Cover and let rise 1 hour until doubled. Punch dough down; divide in half. Form each half into 12-18 smooth balls, depending on how large you want the rolls to be. Place in a greased (9 inch) round cake pan, cover and let rise. Bake at 400 degrees for 20-25 minutes. Serve hot.

Preparation time: 2 hours 45 minutes   Yield: 2 1/2 - 3 dozen

WHEAT GERM ROLLS

2 pkg. yeast
1/3 c. lukewarm water
1 1/2 c. scalded milk
1/2 c. butter
1/2 c. honey

2 eggs, room temperature,
  lightly beaten
5 - 5 1/2 c. whole wheat flour
1 c. wheat germ
1/2 tsp. salt

    Sprinkle yeast into lukewarm water, stir, and allow to stand for a few minutes until it bubbles. Meanwhile, combine milk, honey, and butter in a medium saucepan. Heat until liquids are very warm; butter doesn't have to melt. Add 3 cups of the flour to the yeast mixture, then the beaten eggs. Add the milk mixture and beat at medium speed for 6 minutes. Cover and let rise until doubled, about 1 hour. Stir dough down. Add wheat germ, salt and rest of flour. Knead until smooth and shiny. (Dough is very sticky; oil hands to knead.) Roll to 1 inch thickness on floured surface and cut with 2 1/2 inch round biscuit cutter. Place on greased cookie sheets, cover and let rise until double, about 40 minutes. Bake at 350 degrees for 25 minutes.

Preparation time: 2 1/2 hours   Yield: 1 1/2 dozen

RYE ROLLS

1 pkg. active dry yeast
2 c. warm water
1 1/2 tsp. salt
1/2 c. melted butter,
  cooled to lukewarm

1/2 c. honey
2 eggs, room temperature
2 c. rye flour
3/4 c. wheat germ
4 1/2 - 5 1/2 c. unbleached flour

    Measure yeast into large, warm bowl. Add water, stirring to dissolve. Then add salt, butter, honey, eggs, wheat germ, rye flour and 2 cups unbleached flour; beat until smooth. Gradually stir in enough flour to make a soft dough. Turn out onto floured surface and knead until smooth and elastic; 8-10 minutes (dough will probably be slightly sticky). Place in greased bowl, turning to grease top. Let rise covered, until double, 1 1/2 hours. Punch dough down. Divide dough in half. Shape each half into 14 smooth round balls. Place in 2 greased (8 inch) round pans. Cover, let rise until doubled, about 1 1/2 hours. Bake at 400 degrees for 20-25 minutes or until golden, making sure rolls in center are done.

Preparation time: 3 1/2 hours   Yield: 28-30 rolls

BUTTERMILK BREAD

6 c. unbleached flour
2 1/2 tsp. salt
3 Tbsp. honey
1/3 c. butter
1 c. buttermilk

1/4 tsp. soda
3/4 c. cold water
1/4 c. lukewarm water
1 pkg. yeast

Dissolve yeast in warm water. Heat buttermilk to the boiling point, but do not boil. Dissolve soda, butter, honey and salt in buttermilk, then add cold water, mixture should now be lukewarm. Add 3 cups flour to the buttermilk mixture and beat well. Add yeast water and beat well. Stir in the remaining flour — enough to make a stiff dough. Cover and let rise until double, about 1 hour. Punch dough down, let rest 10 minutes. Shape into 2 loaves (9 X 5 inches), cover and let rise again until doubled. Bake at 350 degrees for 50 minutes; cool on wire racks.

Preparation time: 2 hours 40 minutes   Yield: 2 loaves

YELLOW CORN MEAL BREAD

6 - 7 c. unbleached white flour
1 Tbsp. salt
1 pkg. yeast
2 c. milk

1/3 c. honey
1/3 c. butter or margarine
2 eggs, room temperature
1 c. stone-ground yellow corn meal

Place 2 cups unbleached flour, salt and yeast in a large bowl. Heat milk, honey and butter or margarine until liquids are very warm (butter does not need to melt). Add gradually to flour mixture and beat on medium speed for 2 minutes. Add eggs and corn meal; beat on high for 2 minutes. Stir in enough flour to make a stiff dough; knead until smooth and elastic. Place in a greased bowl, turning to grease top. Cover and let rise 1 hour, until doubled. Punch dough down, let rest for 15 minutes. Shape to fit 2 greased (9 X 5 inch) loaf pans. Cover and let rise until doubled, about 1 hour. Bake at 375 degrees for 35-40 minutes. Cool on racks and brush with butter.

Preparation time: 3 hours   Yield: 2 loaves

OATMEAL BREAD

1/2 c. warm water
2 pkg. yeast
1 3/4 c. warmed milk
1/4 c. honey

1 Tbsp. salt
3 Tbsp. butter or margarine
5 - 5 1/2 c. unbleached flour
1 c. rolled oats

Measure warm water into large, warm bowl, stir to dissolve. Heat milk, honey, salt and butter until liquids are warm; add to yeast mixture along with 2 cups flour. Beat until smooth, then add 1 cup flour and oats. Beat on high speed for 1 minute. Stir in enough flour to make a soft dough, then knead until smooth. Cover with plastic wrap, then a towel. Let rest 20 minutes. Divide dough in half and shape each half to fit a greased (8 1/2 X 4 1/2 inch) loaf pan. Lightly cover tops with safflower oil to keep from drying out. Cover; refrigerate 2-24 hours. When ready to bake, remove from refrigerator, uncover carefully, and let stand 10 minutes. Bake at 400 degrees for 30-40 minutes.

Preparation time: 2 1/2 hours   Yield: 2 loaves

CHEESE BREAD

7 - 7 1/2 c. unbleached flour
1 Tbsp. salt
2 pkg. yeast
2 c. water

2/3 c. milk
1/3 c. honey
3 c. grated sharp cheese

Mix 2 1/2 cups flour, salt and yeast. Heat milk, water and honey until liquids are very warm. Gradually add to dry ingredients and beat on medium speed 1 minute. Add cheese and 1 cup flour, beat on high speed 1 minute. Stir in enough flour to make a stiff dough, then knead until smooth. Place in a greased bowl, turning to grease top. Cover and let rise until doubled, about 1 hour. Punch dough down; cover and let rest about 15 minutes. Divide dough in half; shape each half to fit a greased (9 X 5 inch) loaf pan. Cover and let rise until doubled, about 1 hour. Bake at 375 degrees for 40 minutes.

Preparation time: 3 hours   Yield: 2 loaves

ANADAMA BREAD

6 1/2 - 7 1/2 c. unbleached flour
1 1/2 c. stone-ground yellow
  corn meal
2 1/2 tsp. salt

2 pkg. yeast
2 1/4 c. very warm tap water
1/3 c. softened butter or margarine
2/3 c. honey

Mix 2 1/2 cups flour, corn meal, salt and yeast. Gradually add tap water and mix until blended. Add butter and honey, beat on medium speed for 2 minutes. Add 1 cup flour; beat on high speed 2 minutes. Stir in enough flour to make a stiff dough; knead until smooth and elastic. Cover and let rise until doubled, 1 hour. Punch dough down, divide in half, and shape loaves to fit 9 X 5 inch loaf pan. Cover and let rise until doubled, about 1 hour. Bake at 375 degrees for 45 minutes.

Preparation time: 3 hours   Yield: 2 loaves

BRAN BREAD

1 c. water
3/4 c. milk
1/2 c. honey
1/3 c. butter or margarine
1 c. unprocessed bran

4 tsp. salt
1/2 c. warm water
2 pkg. yeast
3 c. whole wheat flour
2 1/2 - 3 c. unbleached flour

Combine water, milk, honey, butter, and salt in a saucepan. Heat until nearly boiling; add bran and cool to lukewarm. Dissolve yeast in 1/2 cup warm water, then add lukewarm bran mixture and whole wheat flour. Beat on medium speed for 2 minutes; add enough unbleached flour to make a stiff dough. Knead until smooth; cover and let rise until doubled, about 1 hour. Punch dough down; shape to fit 2 greased (8 1/2 X 4 1/2 inch) pans. Cover and let rise until doubled, about 1 hour. Bake at 400 degrees for 40 minutes.

Preparation time: 3 hours   Yield: 2 loaves

RYE AND ORANGE BREAD

2 3/4 c. very warm water
2 pkg. yeast
1/2 c. honey
4 Tbsp. butter or margarine
4 tsp. salt

3 Tbsp. grated orange peel
3 Tbsp. fructose
2 1/2 c. rye flour
1 1/2 c. whole wheat flour
3 - 4 c. unbleached flour

Dissolve yeast in warm water, then add butter, honey, salt, orange peel, fructose, rye and whole wheat flours. Beat at medium speed 2 minutes. Stir in enough unbleached flour to make a stiff dough. Knead until smooth. Place in greased bowl, turning to grease top. Cover and let rise until doubled, about 1 hour. Punch dough down, shape to fit 2 (9 X 5 inch) greased loaf pans. Cover and let rise until doubled, about 1 hour. Bake at 375 degrees about 40 minutes.

Preparation time: 3 hours   Yield: 2 loaves

GERMAN DARK RYE BREAD

3 c. unbleached flour
1/4 c. cocoa powder
2 pkg. yeast
1 Tbsp. caraway seed
1 Tbsp. salt

Scant 1/2 c. honey
2 Tbsp. butter
3 1/2 c. rye flour
Safflower oil

Place unbleached flour, cocoa, yeast, caraway seed and salt in a large bowl. Stir to mix. Place 2 cups water, honey and butter in a saucepan and heat until liquids are very warm. Add to dry ingredients and mix at low speed until moistened, then beat at high speed 3 minutes. Stir in rye flour, enough to make a soft dough. Knead 8-10 minutes; cover and let rest for 20 minutes. Roll out and shape to fit 2 greased (1 pound) loaf pans. Brush tops lightly with oil and score with a knife. Let rise covered, until doubled, about 1 hour. Bake at 400 degrees for 25 minutes.

Preparation time: 2 hours   Yield: 2 loaves

CRACKED WHEAT BREAD

1 1/2 c. water
1/2 c. milk
1/4 c. butter or margarine
3 Tbsp. honey

5 c. unbleached flour
2 pkg. yeast
4 tsp. salt
1 c. cracked wheat

Place water, milk, butter or margarine and honey in a saucepan. Heat until the liquids are very warm. (Butter does not need to melt.) Meanwhile, combine 2 cups flour, salt and yeast. Add liquids and mix at medium speed for 2 minutes, then add cracked wheat and mix on high speed for 2 minutes. Stir in enough flour to make a soft dough, then knead for 8-10 minutes. Place in a greased bowl, turning to grease top. Cover; let rise for about 1 hour, until doubled. Punch dough down, cover and let rest 15 minutes. Divide dough and shape into 2 loaves. Place in 8 1/2 X 4 1/2 inch loaf pan, let rise covered, until doubled, and bake at 400 degrees for 30 minutes.

Preparation time: 3 hours   Yield: 2 loaves

BUTTERMILK WHEAT BREAD

2 pkg. yeast
1 Tbsp. salt
1/2 tsp. soda
4 c. whole wheat flour
2 c. unbleached flour

2 c. buttermilk
1/2 c. water
1/4 c. honey
2 Tbsp. butter or margarine

Combine yeast, salt, soda, and 2 cups whole wheat flour in large bowl; heat buttermilk, water, honey and butter until liquids are very warm. Pour warm liquids over yeast mixture and mix for 2 minutes on medium speed of mixer. Add 2 cups whole wheat flour, mix, then turn to high speed for 2 minutes. Stir in enough of the unbleached flour to make a stiff dough; turn out and knead until smooth and elastic. Place in greased bowl, turning to grease top and let rise until doubled, 1 1/2 hours. Punch dough down, cover and let rest 15 minutes. Shape to fit 2 (8 1/2 X 4 1/2 inch) greased loaf pans, cover and let rise until doubled, 1 hour. Bake at 375 degrees for 35 minutes.

Preparation time: 3 1/2 hours   Yield: 2 loaves

100% WHOLE WHEAT BREAD

2 pkg. yeast	1 Tbsp. salt
6 c. whole wheat flour	3 Tbsp. butter or margarine
1/4 c. honey	2 c. warm water

Combine yeast, 2 cups whole wheat flour, and salt in a large, warm bowl. Heat honey, butter and water until liquids are very warm, add gradually to yeast mixture. Beat 2 minutes at medium speed, then add 1 1/2 cups flour and beat at high speed 2 minutes. Stir in enough flour to make a soft dough, kneading in flour until dough is stiff and elastic. Place in greased bowl, turning to grease top; cover and let rise until doubled, 1 - 1 1/4 hours. Punch dough down, shape to fit 2 (8 1/2 X 4 1/2 inch) greased loaf pans. Cover and let rise until doubled, about 1 hour. Bake at 350 degrees for 35 minutes. Cool on wire racks.

Preparation time: 3 hours   Yield: 2 loaves

WHOLE WHEAT POTATO BREAD

1 medium potato	1/4 c. honey
1 1/2 c. buttermilk	2 Tbsp. butter
2 pkg. active dry yeast	3 c. unbleached flour
1 Tbsp. salt	3 c. whole wheat flour

Cook potato, skin on, until tender. Peel; set aside. Place buttermilk in a medium saucepan and heat until very warm. Set aside 1/2 cup of buttermilk; soften yeast in that; add salt. Mash potato in remaining buttermilk, then add water to make 2 cups. Add honey and butter, return to heat if necessary to bring mixture to a very warm temperature. Add potato mixture to yeast mixture, mix well. Stir in 2 cups of the unbleached flour and beat at low speed for 1/2 minute; then at high speed for 3 minutes. Cover; let rise until doubled, about 1 hour. Stir dough down; stir in the whole wheat flour and enough of the unbleached flour to make a stiff dough. Knead 8-10 minutes; let rise about 45 minutes. Punch down; let rest 10 minutes, then shape to fit 1 (9 X 5 inch) loaf pan. Cover and let rise about 1 hour. Bake at 375 degrees for 40 minutes.

Preparation time: 3 1/2 hours   Yield: 1 loaf

SALADS

SPINACH-ORANGE SALAD WITH SOUR CREAM DRESSING
(Make enough for one meal — leftovers are not good)

1 (10 oz.) pkg. fresh spinach
2 c. fresh orange sections
3 Tbsp. chopped green onions
  with tops

1 c. sour cream
1 - 2 Tbsp. honey
2 Tbsp. orange juice concentrate
1 Tbsp. grated orange rind

Carefully wash spinach leaves, making sure all sand has been washed off, then drain on paper towels. Remove stems and tear into bite-sized pieces; place in large salad bowl. Add orange sections and green onions and toss to mix. Combine sour cream, honey, orange juice concentrate and grated orange rind. Blend or whip until smooth; pour over salad just before serving, and toss.

Preparation time: 30 minutes   Yield: 8 servings

ASPARAGUS MOUSSE
Reprinted from the Starr Cookbook
by permission of WATE-TV, Knoxville, Tn.

1 can cut green asparagus
1/2 tsp. salt
1/2 c. mayonnaise*
1/2 c. cream, whipped

2 Tbsp. gelatin
1/4 c. cold water
4 Tbsp. lemon juice
2 Tbsp. blanched almonds

Heat liquid from asparagus and pour over gelatin which has been soaked in water. Cool, then fold in mayonnaise, whipped cream, salt, lemon juice and almonds. Chill; add asparagus when mixture begins to thicken. Pour into mold, cover and chill.

Preparation time: 30 minutes   Yield: 6 - 8 servings

MARINATED CUCUMBERS & ONIONS

1 c. safflower oil
1/2 c. honey
1/2 c. apple cider vinegar

1/2 tsp. dill weed
2 c. peeled, sliced cucumbers
1/2 onion, sliced thin

Stir together oil, honey, vinegar and dill weed until well mixed. Marinate cucumbers and onions for several hours or overnight.

Preparation time: 10 minutes +   Yield: 2 1/2 cups
                overnight

STUFFED TOMATOES

4 large tomatoes
1 pkg. Italian style frozen
  vegetables
1/2 c. mayonnaise*

1 tsp. lemon juice
1/2 tsp. Italian seasoning
1/4 tsp. garlic salt
1/2 c. slivered almonds

Wash tomatoes; remove stem and core; cut in quarters but do not cut all the way through. Steam vegetables 2-3 minutes in vegetable steamer; blanch with cold water. Combine vegetables with mayonnaise and seasonings; fold in almonds last. Stuff tomatoes with vegetable salad; serve on lettuce leaves.

Preparation time: 20 minutes   Yield: 4 servings

SEASONLESS VEGETABLE SALAD

2 c. chopped carrots
2 c. chopped celery
1 c. diced, peeled cucumber
1/2 c. chopped green pepper
1/2 c. sliced radishes

1 1/2 c. creamed cottage cheese
1/2 c. mayonnaise*
1 Tbsp. dried onion
1 1/2 tsp. salt

Combine all vegetables; mix cottage cheese, mayonnaise, onion and salt and toss with vegetables. Chill thoroughly.

Preparation time: 30 minutes   Yield: 6 - 8 servings

MARINATED BROCCOLI SALAD

1 bunch fresh broccoli
3/4 c. safflower oil
1/4 c. lemon juice
2/3 c. light cream
1 Tbsp. honey
1 tsp. salt

1 tsp. dried onion
1/2 tsp. dried garlic
1/2 tsp. paprika
1/4 tsp. white pepper
3 tomatoes

Wash broccoli, break off flowerets to use in salad. Steam for 3 minutes in vegetable steamer. (Discard the stems or cook and serve.) Pour oil, lemon juice, cream, honey, salt, onion, garlic, paprika and pepper in blender, cover and mix until smooth. Marinate broccoli flowerets in dressing overnight. Just before serving, dice tomatoes and toss.

Preparation time: 20 minutes +   Yield: 4 - 5 servings
           overnight

CUCUMBER SALAD

1 c. cucumber, unpeeled and
   thinly sliced
1 small head lettuce
1/2 c. thinly sliced red radishes
1/4 c. thinly sliced onion
1/2 c. sour cream

1 Tbsp. apple cider vinegar
1 Tbsp. mustard
1 Tbsp. chives
1 Tbsp. honey
1/2 tsp. salt

Cut up vegetables and place in large bowl. Mix vinegar and spices with sour cream and pour over salad; stir well. Chill and serve.

Preparation time: 15 minutes   Yield: 4 - 6 servings

POTATO-CHEESE SALAD

6 - 7 baking potatoes
4 oz. Blue cheese
2 c. celery
1/4 c. chopped onions
2 chopped, hard-boiled eggs
1/2 c. mayonnaise*

1/2 c. sour cream
3 Tbsp. apple cider vinegar
1 Tbsp. honey
Salt and pepper to taste
Paprika

Boil potatoes whole, skins on. Boil eggs with potatoes for 10 minutes; remove. Chop celery and onions; crumble cheese; skin and chop potatoes and combine with celery mixture. Add diced eggs. Mix mayonnaise and sour cream; add honey and vinegar, stirring to mix well. Pour over salad and fold in carefully; salt and pepper to taste. Sprinkle with paprika; chill.

Preparation time: 30 minutes   Yield: 6 servings

TANGY ZUCCHINI SALAD

1 c. apple cider vinegar
3/4 c. safflower oil
2 Tbsp. honey
1 tsp. salt
1 1/2 tsp. basil leaves

1/4 tsp. garlic powder
Dash pepper
4 c. sliced zucchini
3/4 c. green onion tops (only)
4 tomatoes, cut in eighths

Mix vinegar, oil, salt, honey, basil, garlic powder, and pepper in a container with a tight fitting lid. Shake well. Steam zucchini, unpeeled and sliced, in vegetable steamer for 2 minutes only; place in container with dressing, and refrigerate overnight.

To serve, wash tomatoes and cut in fourths. Form a circle around the edge of plate with tomatoes, place drained zucchini in the center, and top with onion tops. Drizzle 2 tablespoons dressing over all.

Preparation time: overnight   Yield: 6 servings

GREEN PEA SALAD

1/3 c. milk
1/3 c. mayonnaise*
1 Tbsp. lemon juice
1 Tbsp. prepared horseradish
Dash of salt

1 (10-oz.) pkg. of frozen
   green peas
2 Tbsp. green onion
2 Tbsp. chopped celery
Salt to taste

Combine milk, mayonnaise, lemon juice, horseradish and a dash of salt in blender. Cover and process until creamy, about 20-30 seconds. Empty peas into a saucepan, cover with very hot water and close lid. Allow to stand for 3 minutes, then pour off hot water and rinse with cold water. Add onion and celery, then dressing. Salt to taste and serve icy cold.

Preparation time: 10 minutes   Yield: 4 servings

BROCCOLI AND CAULIFLOWER SALAD

1 bunch fresh broccoli
1 head fresh cauliflower

1 c. French Dressing*

Wash broccoli and cauliflower, separate into tiny flowerets, using just enough stem to hold the flower on. Combine in large bowl; add dressing; toss and chill.

Preparation time: 10 minutes   Yield: 4 servings

CUCUMBERS IN SOUR CREAM
Reprinted from the Starr Cookbook
by permission of WATE-TV, Knoxville, Tn.

2 c. thinly sliced cucumbers
Salt
Ice
2/3 c. sour cream
1 Tbsp. honey

Dash of Tabasco sauce
Cider vinegar
1 1/2 tsp. prepared mustard
1 Tbsp. chopped chives

Peel and slice cucumbers. Cover with salt and let stand 1 hour. Drain; combine all other ingredients except vinegar. Add vinegar to sauce, thinning to desired consistency. Combine cucumbers and dressings; serve icy cold.

Preparation time: 1 1/2 hours   Yield: 3 cups

MARINATED VEGETABLE SALAD

3/4 c. safflower oil
3/4 c. apple cider vinegar
1/2 c. honey

2 cans French green beans
1 can small early peas
1 onion

Mix oil, vinegar and honey. Drain vegetables and slice onion into thin slices, separating into rings. Combine vegetables with oil mixture and chill. Will keep 2 weeks.

Preparation time: 15 minutes   Yield: 8 servings

SEVEN VEGETABLE SALAD

1 can English peas
1 can kidney beans
1 c. chopped onion
1 1/2 c. chopped celery
3 c. chopped cabbage,
   as for slaw
1 chopped green pepper

4 - 5 tomatoes
1 Tbsp. salt
1/2 tsp. white pepper
1 Tbsp. honey
2 Tbsp. apple cider vinegar
1/2 c. mayonnaise*

Combine vegetables, drain well. Add seasonings and mayonnaise, chill.

Preparation time: 30 minutes   Yield: 1/2 gallon salad

WINTER CITRUS SALAD

2 pink grapefruit
2 - 3 naval oranges
3 pears
1/2 c. concord grapes
1 c. plain yogurt

2 Tbsp. orange-pineapple juice
   concentrate
2 Tbsp. mayonnaise*
1 Tbsp. orange rind
1/2 c. large walnut pieces

Section oranges; section and seed grapefruit. Peel pears, and slice into small chunks. Slice and seed grapes. Place fruits in large bowl. Combine yogurt, juice concentrate, mayonnaise and orange peel in blender. Process until smooth; pour over fruit. Refrigerate until serving — at least for 30 minutes. Just before serving, add walnuts and stir well.

Preparation time: 1 hour   Yield: 6 servings

COMBINATION CITRUS SALAD
(Must be eaten at one meal, leftovers are not good.)

1 head Romaine or leaf lettuce
3 pink grapefruit
6 navel oranges
1 c. plain yogurt
2 Tbsp. lemon juice

1 - 2 Tbsp. honey
1 Tbsp. lemon peel
1/4 tsp. vanilla
Dash salt
1/2 c. chopped walnuts

Wash lettuce carefully; pat dry. Tear into small pieces and place in large salad bowl. Section grapefruit; peel and slice oranges crosswise, separating into sections; toss with lettuce. Combine yogurt, lemon juice, honey, lemon peel, vanilla, and dash salt. Blend or whip until smooth; pour over salad just before serving and toss. Sprinkle with 1/2 cup chopped walnuts.

Preparation time: 30 minutes   Yield: 8 servings

CHERRY-CHEESE SALAD

1 bag frozen unsweetened
  cherries
1/3 c. fructose
2 pkg. unflavored gelatin
1 (15 1/2 oz.) can unsweetened
  pineapple

2 Tbsp. lemon juice
2 Tbsp. lime juice
1/2 c. honey
2 c. cottage cheese
1/3 c. mayonnaise*
1/4 c. slivered almonds

Combine cherries and fructose; allow to stand until thawed and sweetened. Drain juice from cherries and pineapple to make 1 1/2 cups. Soften gelatin in juice, then stir over hot water until dissolved. (Or microwave 1 minute.) Fold cottage cheese, mayonnaise, lemon and lime juice and honey into gelatin mixture; pour into a 13 X 9 inch pan. Add cherries and almonds; arrange pineapple slices on top; chill until firm.

Preparation time: 20 minutes +   Yield: 8 servings
                chill time

"UNMOLDED" GELATIN SALAD

1 (12 oz.) carton creamed
   cottage cheese
2 (3 oz.) pkg. cream cheese,
   softened
2 tsp. unflavored gelatin
1/4 c. cold water
1/4 tsp. salt
2 Tbsp. chives

1 c. red grapes, seeded and halved,
   or green grapes in season
1/2 c. chopped nuts
1 c. heavy cream, whipped and
   unsweetened
1 can unsweetened pineapple
   slices
Chef style French dressing*

Combine cheeses and mix well. Soften gelatin in cold water, then stir over hot water until dissolved. (Or, place in microwave on "high" for 30 seconds.) Stir gelatin mixture and salt, chives, grapes, nuts and cream into cheeses. Turn into a 6 1/2 X 10 inch oblong dish and top with pineapple slices, placing a nut in the center of each slice. Refrigerate several hours or overnight. Serve a square with a pineapple slice on top for each serving, top with Chef style French dressing.

Preparation time: 20 minutes   Yield: 8 servings

ORANGE-GRAPEFRUIT SALAD WITH AVOCADO DRESSING

4 large seedless oranges
1 large pink grapefruit
1/2 c. orange juice
1/2 lemon, peeled and seeded

1/4 tsp. salt
1 Tbsp. mayonnaise*
1 cubed, ripe avocado
1 - 2 Tbsp. honey

Section oranges and grapefruit; place in bowl. Combine orange juice, lemon, salt, mayonnaise and avocado in blender; mix until smooth. Add 1 - 2 tablespoons honey to taste and pour over salad, stirring to coat. Cover and chill until serving time.

Preparation time: 20 minutes   Yield: 4 servings, 1/2 cup each

STUFFED PEAR SALAD

4 ripe pears
1 (4 oz.) carton cream cheese,
  room temperature
1 Tbsp. cream or evaporated milk
1/8 tsp. almond extract

1/8 tsp. vanilla extract
1 - 2 Tbsp. honey
1/4 c. golden raisins
1 Tbsp. slivered almonds (optional)

Peel and halve pears, removing core. Whip cream cheese with cream and flavorings; add honey to taste, about 1 tablespoon, and whip for 1 minute on high speed of mixer. Stir in raisins and top each pear half with a scoop of cheese mixture. Sprinkle almonds on top if desired and serve on a bed of leaf lettuce.

Preparation time: 10 minutes   Yield: 4 - 6 servings

CREAMY FRUIT SALAD

1 (3 oz.) carton cream cheese
1/3 c. mayonnaise*
1/2 pt. heavy cream, whipped
1/4 tsp. vanilla
1 lb. red grapes, seeded and halved

2 bananas
1 (15 oz.) can crushed pineapple
  in its own juice
3/4 c. walnuts, broken coarsely

Whip cream; add to cream cheese, mayonnaise and vanilla. Seed grapes, slice bananas and chop walnuts. Add to creamy mixture along with drained pineapple. May be chilled or frozen.
Salad is better if made up early in the day or overnight and allowed to stand 8-10 hours.

Preparation time: 30 minutes   Yield: 8 - 10 servings

POPPY SEED DRESSING ON FRESH FRUIT SALAD

2 c. fresh strawberries
1 c. fresh peaches
2 bananas
1 (15 1/2 oz.) can chunk
  pineapple in own juice
1/4 c. orange juice

1/4 c. pineapple juice
1/4 c. lemon juice
1/2 c. honey
2 eggs
1/2 c. heavy cream, whipped
2 Tbsp. poppy seed

Slice and combine fruits, cover and refrigerate. Bring juices to a boil; add honey. Stir small amount of hot mixture into eggs, then return to pan. Cook and stir until slightly thickened, about 30 minutes. Remove from heat and fold in cream and poppy seed. Pour over salad; chill.

Preparation time: 30 minutes   Yield: 6 servings

GRAPEFRUIT COMPOTE

3/4 c. safflower oil
1/3 c. apple cider vinegar
2 Tbsp. honey
1 1/2 tsp. minced onion
3/4 tsp. salt

1/2 tsp. paprika
1/4 tsp. dry mustard
1/8 tsp. black pepper
3 c. white grapefruit sections
6 oz. can grapefruit juice concentrate

Combine all ingredients except grapefruit and grapefruit juice concentrate in blender and whirl until smooth. Blend with grapefruit juice concentrate, pour over sections and chill.

Preparation time: 10 minutes   Yield: 1 quart

CARROT AND RAISIN SALAD

2 c. shredded carrots
1 apple, peeled and shredded
2 apples, unpeeled and diced
1/4 c. mayonnaise*

1/4 c. apple juice concentrate
1/2 tsp. lemon juice
Dash salt
3/4 c. raisins

Combine all ingredients except raisins; stir well; cover and chill until serving time. Add raisins just before serving.

Preparation time: 10 minutes   Yield: 4 servings

CREAMY CRANBERRY SALAD

1 (3 oz.) pkg. cream cheese
1 Tbsp. mayonnaise*
1 c. whipping cream
2 Tbsp. fructose

1 (8 oz.) can crushed pineapple,
   in its own juice
2 c. whole berry cranberry sauce*
1/2 c. slivered almonds

Soften cream cheese and blend in mayonnaise. Whip cream, sweetening with 2 tablespoons fructose, then stir into cheese mixture. Combine cranberry sauce, pineapple and almonds; pour whipped cream dressing over all. May freeze, or chill 24 hours, then serve.

Preparation time: 15 minutes +   Y ield: 12 servings
                  24 hours

WINTER CRANBERRY SALAD

1 (16 oz.) pkg. fresh or frozen
  cranberries
1 c. fructose
2 c. seeded white grapes

1 c. pecan meats
1 (15 oz.) can unsweetened, crushed
  pineapple, drained
1 c. half & half

Wash cranberries and drain. Process in blender until berries are coarsely chopped, place in bowl and cover with fructose. Allow to stand overnight. Add grapes, pecans and drained pineapple to cranberries. Add cream and a pinch of salt. Stir well and serve.

Preparation time: overnight   Yield: 6 - 8 servings

WALDORF SALAD

2 large tart apples
1 c. chopped celery
1 c. walnuts
1/2 c. raisins

1 tsp. lemon juice
1/2 c. plain yogurt
3 Tbsp. apple juice concentrate
1 Tbsp. mayonnaise*

Wash, core and dice apples, leaving peeling on. Combine with celery, walnuts and raisins; sprinkle with lemon juice. Stir yogurt, apple juice concentrate, and mayonnaise together until smooth. Toss with salad; cover and refrigerate, or serve at once.

Preparation time: 10 minutes   Yield: 6 servings

FAVORITE SUMMER SALAD

1/2 red watermelon
1 large honeydew melon
2 ripe canteloupes

3 c. green grapes
2 c. fresh cherries, pitted

The night before serving, halve watermelon lengthwise and make a decorative pattern around the cut edge. Using melon ball scoop, make melon balls out of watermelon, honeydew, and canteloupe meat. Place in a large covered container and fold in grapes and cherries. Cover and re-frigerate. Saving the scraps from the melons for later use, discard all shells except the decorated watermelon shell. Drain juices from it; cover and re-frigerate. Just before serving, pour fruits into watermelon shell. Save juices to pour 1 cup over fruits. Add remaining juices to any summer drink.

Preparation time: 1 hour   Yield: 8 - 10 servings

COLD FRUIT SOUP

2 c. orange juice
2 Tbsp. cornstarch
1 Tbsp. honey
2 bananas

1 c. green grapes
1 1/2 c. unsweetened pineapple
  chunks, drained
1 pt. strawberries

Combine orange juice and cornstarch; mix until smooth; then add honey. Heat to boiling point; remove to bowl. Slice fruits and put into "soup stock"; cover and chill overnight.

Preparation time: 20 minutes   Yield: 6 - 8 servings

CHILLED AMBROSIA

4 c. fresh orange sections
1 c. unsweetened coconut

1/3 c. orange-pineapple juice
3 Tbsp. fructose

Combine all ingredients; chill.

Preparation time: 15 minutes   Yield: 6 servings

HEALTHY HEAVENLY HASH

1 (15 1/2 oz.) can unsweetened
  pineapple chunks
2 ripe bananas, sliced
1/2 c. diced celery
1/2 c. grated sharp cheese
1/2 c. broken nutmeats

2 eggs
3 Tbsp. unbleached flour
2 Tbsp. apple cider vinegar
Pinch of salt
1/2 pt. heavy cream, whipped
3 Tbsp. fructose

Drain pineapple, reserving juice. Cut chunks in half; slice bananas and combine with celery, cheese and nuts. Cover and set aside. Combine reserved pineapple juice, eggs, flour, vinegar and salt. Beat with mixer or blend until smooth. Cook and stir over medium heat until thickened; cool slightly, then fold in whipped cream sweetened with fructose. Stir dressing into salad and cover; chill for 24 hours.

Preparation time: 24 hours   Yield: 6 servings

NUTTY CHICKEN SALAD

2 c. cooked, cubed chicken
1/2 c. chopped celery
1/2 c. coarsely ground peanuts

1/4 c. crushed pineapple in its own
  juice, drained
1/4 c. mayonnaise*
Salt and pepper to taste

Mix all ingredients together, season to taste and chill.

Preparation time: 15 minutes   Yield: 2 1/2 cups salad

HOT TURKEY SALAD

2 c. cubed, cooked turkey
2 c. chopped celery
1/2 c. slivered almonds
4 slices American or Colby
  cheese
2 Tbsp. lemon juice

1 c. mayonnaise*
1/2 tsp. salt
2 Tbsp. chopped green onion
Crushed natural style potato
  chips

Mix turkey, celery, and almonds in a casserole dish. Combine lemon juice, mayonnaise, salt, and onions and pour over turkey. Top with cheese slices, then with crushed potato chips. Bake 20 minutes in a 450 degree oven.

Preparation time: 30 minutes   Yield: 6 servings

TURKEY-CUCUMBER SALAD

2 c. cooked turkey, chopped
1 c. chopped, peeled cucumber
1/2 c. chopped celery
1/2 c. mayonnaise*

1/2 c. slivered almonds
1 Tbsp. lemon juice
1/4 tsp. paprika
Salt and pepper to taste

Combine turkey, cucumber, celery and mayonnaise in a large bowl. Toss until mayonnaise coats all, then add lemon juice and seasonings. Add almonds and stir well; serve icy cold.

Preparation time: 15 minutes   Yield: 4 cups salad

1 1/2 lb. lean ground beef
2 Tbsp. chili powder
1 Tbsp. dried onion
1 Tbsp. whole wheat flour
1 tsp. salt
1/4 tsp. pepper

1/8 - 1/4 tsp. Tabasco sauce
2 Tbsp. honey
1 c. water
8 c. assorted torn salad greens
2 c. chopped tomatoes
2 c. shredded Cheddar cheese

Brown ground beef; combine dry seasonings and stir into beef. Add honey and water; simmer uncovered for ten minutes. Combine torn salad greens, chopped tomatoes and shredded cheese; toss well to mix. To serve, place salad greens in bowl and top with desired hot meat mixture. Mix well; serve with Doritos plain taco chips.

Preparation time: 30 minutes   Yield: 6 servings

SALMON FRUIT SALAD

1 c. boned, cooked salmon
1/3 c. mayonnaise*
3 Tbsp. apple juice concentrate
2 c. unpeeled, diced apples

1/2 c. raisins
1/2 c. broken walnuts
1/2 c. diced celery
1/4 c. apple juice concentrate

Combine salmon, mayonnaise and 3 tablespoons apple juice concentrate. Stir well, cover and chill. Meanwhile, mix apples, walnuts, raisins and celery. Add to salmon; pour 1/4 cup apple juice concentrate over all; stir and chill.

Preparation time: 15 minutes   Yield: 6 servings

SHRIMP SALAD

1 (8 oz.) pkg. cream cheese
1/2 c. mayonnaise*
1 Tbsp. lemon juice
1 Tbsp. horseradish mustard
1 Tbsp. onion juice
1 Tbsp. tangy catsup*

Salt and cayenne to taste
2 Tbsp. green onions and tops
2 c. diced celery
1 c. green fresh or frozen peas[1]
10 oz. cooked shrimp

Whip cream cheese, mayonnaise, lemon juice, mustard, onion juice, catsup, salt and cayenne until light, fold in shrimp, peas, celery and green onions. Cover and chill.

Preparation time: 15 minutes   Yield: 6 servings
[1] If fresh peas are used, steam 3 minutes only, then quick chill. If frozen peas are used soak in hot water for 4 minutes, then drain and use.

MOLDED TUNA SALAD

1 (12 oz.) can tuna, rinsed and
  drained
2 hard boiled eggs, chopped
1/2 c. diced celery
1/3 chopped pickles*
2 Tbsp. minced onion

1 tsp. salt
1/4 tsp. paprika
1/4 tsp. pepper
1 envelope unflavored gelatin
1 c. cold water
1 c. mayonnaise*

Combine drained tuna, chopped hard boiled eggs, celery, pickles, onion and seasonings. Soften gelatin in cold water; stir over hot water until dissolved. (Or, place in a microwave oven on "high" for 1 minute.) Stir into mayonnaise with wire whip or fork, until smooth. Pour gelatin mixture into tuna salad and chill for several hours.

This doesn't make a really firm molded salad, but it will unmold on lettuce and hold its shape.

Preparation time: 20 minutes   Yield: 4 - 6 servings

VEGETABLES

SPINACH CASSEROLE

2 (10 oz.) pkg. frozen,
  chopped spinach
2 c. creamed cottage cheese
1 1/2 c. cubed American cheese

3 beaten eggs
1/4 c. whole wheat flour
1/4 c. melted butter
1 tsp. salt

    Cook spinach and drain. Combine with other ingredients and bake, covered, 1/2 hour at 400 degrees.

Preparation time: 45 minutes   Yield: 6 servings

GREEN RICE

3 c. cooked brown rice
1 1/3 c. evaporated milk
1/2 c. safflower oil
1/4 c. minced onion
1/2 c. chopped carrots

1 (10 oz.) pkg. cooked spinach,
  drained
1 c. shredded sharp cheese
2 tsp. salt
1/4 tsp. pepper

    Combine ingredients and bake, covered, 45-55 minutes at 350 degrees.

Preparation time: 1 hour   Yield: 6 servings

CREAMED CORN

4 c. fresh or frozen corn
3 pieces salt pork or 2
  teaspoons bacon fat from
  fresh hickory-smoked bacon
1/2 c. diced onions

2 Tbsp. butter or margarine
1 c. half & half or evaporated
  milk
1/2 tsp. salt
1/4 tsp. pepper

    Steam corn in vegetable steamer until tender, about 5 minutes. Meanwhile, brown salt pork for a few minutes until 2 teaspoons of fat is in the skillet; remove. Place onions in skillet with fat and add butter; sauté for 5 minutes or until tender. Add corn, cream and seasonings; cover and cook on low heat for 10 minutes.

Preparation time: 20 minutes   Yield: 6 servings

PEAS AND CORN IN SOUR CREAM

1 (10 oz.) pkg. frozen corn
1 (10 oz.) pkg. frozen peas
2 Tbsp. butter or margarine
1/2 c. chopped onion
1/2 c. chopped celery

1 tsp. dried parsley
1 tsp. salt
1 tsp. lemon juice
1/4 tsp. white pepper
1 c. sour cream

Steam peas and corn together in vegetable steamer for about 5-7 minutes. Meanwhile, sauté onions and celery in butter, then combine with remaining ingredients. Drain cooked vegetables; stir in sauce and heat to the boiling point (do not boil).

Preparation time: 10 minutes   Yield: 6 servings

DILLED BEANS

2 (10 oz.) pkg. frozen French
  green beans
1/2 c. light cream
1/2 c. sour cream

1 tsp. dill weed
1 Tbsp. lemon juice
1/2 tsp. salt
1/4 tsp. white pepper

Steam beans in vegetable steamer for 5 minutes; drain. Combine remaining ingredients with beans and heat until warm throughout. (Do not boil.)

Preparation time: 15 minutes   Yield: 6 servings

STUFFED EGGPLANT

1 large eggplant
1 tsp. salt
1/4 c. butter or margarine
1/2 c. chopped celery
1/2 c. chopped onion
1/4 c. chopped green pepper

1/2 c. bread crumbs from homemade
  bread
2 eggs
1/2 tsp. salt
1/4 tsp. pepper
1/4 c. wheat germ
1/4 c. melted butter or margarine

Slice eggplant lengthwise, removing pulp. Soak shell in 1 teaspoon salt and water to cover for 1 hour. Boil pulp gently, covered, until tender. Sauté celery, onion and pepper in butter for 5 minutes. Add crumbs, eggs, salt and pepper and mix well. Mash cooked eggplant with fork and add to stuffing. Stuff shells; top with melted butter and wheat germ. Bake 30 minutes at 350 degrees.

Preparation time: 1 3/4 hours   Yield: 4 servings

CAULIFLOWER AMANDINE

1 head cauliflower
4 Tbsp. butter
2 Tbsp. oat flour or other
   whole grain flour
1 1/2 c. milk

1/2 tsp. nutmeg
1/4 tsp. mace
1/4 tsp. white pepper
1/2 tsp. salt
1/2 c. chopped or slivered almonds

Break cauliflower into flowerets; cook in vegetable steamer 8-10 minutes. Meanwhile, melt 2 tablespoons butter in saucepan. Place flour and seasonings along with milk in blender; whirl until smooth. Add to butter and stir, cooking until mixture bubbles and thickens. Place cauliflower in a buttered 1 quart casserole and cover with cream sauce, then sprinkle with almonds. Top with a few grains of nutmeg and bake,[2] covered, for 20 minutes at 350 degrees.

Preparation time: 40 minutes
[2] Or microwave for 6-8 minutes.

Yield: 4 servings

CAULIFLOWER WITH SOUR CREAM SAUCE

1 head fresh cauliflower
4 Tbsp. butter or margarine
2 Tbsp. whole wheat flour
1 c. chicken stock
Dash nutmeg
1 Tbsp. parsley

1 tsp. dried onion
1/2 tsp. salt
1/4 tsp. pepper
1/2 c. sour cream
1/2 c. almonds, slivered

Steam cauliflower for 6-7 minutes in vegetable steamer. Melt butter, stir in flour and cook for a minute or so, stirring until mixture leaves the sides of skillet. Add chicken stock, cooking and stirring until thickened. Add seasonings and sour cream, then almonds. Pour over cauliflower and serve piping hot.

Preparation time: 15 minutes

Yield: 4-6 servings

ZUCCHINI CHEESE PUFF

3 c. sliced zucchini
2 Tbsp. whole wheat flour
1/2 tsp. salt
1 1/2 c. shredded Swiss cheese
3/4 c. sour cream

2 eggs, room temperature
1/4 c. wheat germ
1 Tbsp. chives
1/8 tsp. pepper
2 Tbsp. Parmesan cheese

Steam zucchini in vegetable steamer for 3 minutes; remove to 1 1/2 quart casserole dish. Sprinkle zucchini with flour, salt, and 1 cup Swiss cheese. Combine sour cream and egg yolks, wheat germ, chives and pepper, mix well. Beat egg whites until stiff and fold into sour cream mixture. Pour on top zucchini, top with remaining Swiss cheese and Parmesan cheese. Bake at 375 degrees for 35-40 minutes. Serve immediately.

Preparation time: 1 hour   Yield: 6 servings

STUFFED ZUCCHINI SQUASH

2 large zucchini
2 Tbsp. butter or margarine
1/2 c. chopped onion
1 c. chopped, unpeeled tomato
1 c. grated sharp cheese

1/2 c. slivered almonds
1/2 tsp. garlic salt
1/4 tsp. black pepper
1/4 c. Parmesan cheese

Boil whole zucchini for 10 minutes; cover with cold water. Meanwhile, melt butter; sauté onion for 5 minutes in butter. Stir in other ingredients except Parmesan cheese; cook and stir over medium heat for 2 or 3 minutes. (Cheese does not have to melt.) Set aside. Halve zucchini lengthwise; remove seeds (seeds may be added to stuffing or discarded as desired). Stuff with tomato mixture and top with Parmesan cheese. Bake at 425 degrees for 5 minutes, or until cheese is bubbly and golden.

Preparation time: 25 minutes   Yield: 4 generous servings

AUNT FANNY'S BAKER SQUASH CASSEROLE

3 lb. small yellow squash
1/4 c. butter
1 1/2 c. chopped onion
2 large eggs

Salt and pepper to taste
1/2 c. milk
3/4 c. shredded sharp cheese
1/2 c. wheat germ

Wash squash; slice into small pieces and cook until tender. Drain, and add butter, onion, cheese, eggs, wheat germ, milk, and seasonings. Bake for 20-25 minutes, until set, in a 450 degree oven.

Preparation time: 20 minutes   Yield: 8 - 10 servings

BAKED ZUCCHINI ALMONDINE

4 c. grated zucchini
1 1/4 c. grated Cheddar cheese
1 c. bread crumbs (from homemade bread)
1/2 c. slivered almonds
3 Tbsp. butter or margarine
3/4 c. chopped onion

1/4 tsp. garlic powder
1 tsp. salt
1/4 tsp. thyme
1/4 tsp. white pepper
2 eggs
1/2 c. milk

Combine zucchini, 1 cup cheese and bread crumbs. Turn into casserole dish and set aside. Sauté onion and garlic in butter; add other seasonings and blend into zucchini. Combine milk and eggs; pour over zucchini, stirring to moisten. Top with remaining cheese and bake at 350 degrees for 30 minutes.

Preparation time: 40 minutes   Yield: 6 servings

DRESSED-UP BEANS

2 c. fresh green beans[3]
2 c. fresh garden peas
2 c. fresh limas
1 c. mayonnaise*
2 hard boiled eggs

1 medium onion, cut in cubes
1 tsp. mustard
2 tsp. lemon juice
Several dashes of Tabasco sauce

Cook vegetables and season with salt. Place mayonnaise and eggs in blender; whirl until mixed. Add onion pieces while motor is running. Add mustard and lemon juice and pour over piping hot vegetables. Serve immediately.

Preparation time: 40 minutes   Yield: 8-10 servings
[3] Or use frozen if fresh are unavailable.

FRENCH GREEN BEAN BAKE

2 (10 oz.) pkg. frozen French
  green beans
1 c. grated Swiss cheese
3 Tbsp. butter or margarine
1/4 c. chopped onion
2 Tbsp. whole wheat flour

1 tsp. salt
1/4 tsp. pepper
1 tsp. honey
1 c. yogurt
1/4 c. wheat germ
2 Tbsp. butter or margarine, melted

Steam beans in vegetable steamer until done; set aside. Meanwhile, melt butter and sauté onions. Stir in flour and seasonings. Add yogurt, then cook and stir until thickened. Add cheese and stir until melted. Combine beans and sauce; turn into casserole dish. Top with melted butter and wheat germ; bake at 350 degrees for 25-30 minutes.

Preparation time: 45 minutes   Yield: 4 - 6 servings

BROCCOLI SOUFFLÉ
Reprinted from the Starr Cookbook
by permission of WATE-TV, Knoxville, Tn.

3 Tbsp. butter
3 Tbsp. unbleached flour
1 c. milk
1/4 tsp. salt
1/8 tsp. pepper
8 oz. grated sharp cheese

1 (10 oz.) pkg. frozen broccoli
  pieces, thawed
1/2 c. finely chopped onion
3 well beaten egg yolks
3 stiffly beaten egg whites

Make a cream sauce by melting butter and stirring in flour and seasonings. Then add milk, cooking and stirring until thickened. Add cheese and stir until it melts. Add onion, broccoli and egg yolks, then carefully fold in beaten egg whites. Turn into a well-buttered 2 quart soufflé dish and bake for 45-50 minutes at 350 degrees. Serve immediately.

Preparation time: 1 hour   Yield: 6 servings

SPINACH SOUFFLÉ

3 (10 oz.) pkg. frozen chopped
  spinach
2 Tbsp. butter or margarine
3 Tbsp. whole wheat flour
1 1/2 c. milk
1 1/2 c. cubed Cheddar cheese

1 Tbsp. minced onion
1 tsp. salt
1/2 tsp. nutmeg
3 beaten eggs
1/4 c. chopped nuts (optional)

Cook spinach in vegetable steamer; drain well. Melt butter in saucepan. Combine flour, milk and cheese in blender; whirl until smooth. Pour into saucepan containing butter; cook and stir until bubbly. Add onion, salt and nutmeg, then beaten eggs. Turn into greased casserole dish and top with walnuts. Bake at 350 degrees[4] until set, 50-55 minutes.

Preparation time: 1 1/4 hours   Yield: 8 servings
[4] Or, microwave on "high" for 15 minutes.

SPINACH SURPRISE

2 boxes frozen, chopped
  spinach
1/2 c. raisins

1/2 c. slivered almonds
2 Tbsp. butter
Salt to taste

Cook spinach; drain thoroughly. Just before serving, add raisins, butter and almonds and salt to taste. Return to heat just long enough to warm the added ingredients.

Preparation time: 20 minutes   Yield: 4 - 6 servings

BAKED SPINACH

1 c. fresh bread cubes (3 slices)
1/2 c. butter or margarine
2 (10 oz.) pkg. frozen, chopped
  spinach
1 medium onion, chopped
4 oz. shredded Muenster cheese
2 tsp. salt

1/8 tsp. pepper
1/8 tsp. nutmeg
1/4 c. unbleached flour
1 c. milk
1/3 c. grated Parmesan cheese
4 eggs, room temperature

Sauté bread cubes in 2 tablespoons of butter until golden; set aside. Sauté onion in 2 more tablespoons of butter; set aside. Cook spinach according to package directions; drain well. Add onion, Muenster cheese, salt, pepper, nutmeg and bread cubes. Place in lightly greased 6-cup soufflé or baking dish. Melt remaining butter in a small saucepan; add flour and cook, stirring constantly until bubbly. Add milk slowly, and continue stirring and cooking until sauce bubbles for 1 minute. Stir in Parmesan cheese; salt lightly. Separate eggs, beat yolks until thick and fluffy; stir into cream sauce. Then beat whites until very stiff and fold carefully into cream sauce. Spoon over spinach. Bake at 375 degrees for 45 minutes.

Preparation time: 1 1/2 hours   Yield: 8 servings.

CURRIED PEAS

1 (10 oz.) pkg. frozen green peas
  (or 2 c. fresh peas)
1/2 tsp. salt

1/2 tsp. curry powder
2 Tbsp. butter

Cook peas in vegetable steamer until just tender. Place in bowl and cover. Melt butter; add salt and curry powder. Stir into peas and serve.

Preparation time: 10 minutes   Yield: 4 servings

PARSLEYED RICE

1 c. uncooked brown rice
1/3 c. safflower oil
1 c. evaporated milk
1 1/2 c. cubed sharp cheese
1 egg

1 large onion, cubed
1 bunch ground parsley.
1 green pepper, cut into pieces
1 Tbsp. salt

Cook rice and drain. Place oil, milk, egg and salt in blender. With motor running, add cubed onion, cheese, pepper pieces and parsley leaves a little at a time, blending to mix. Pour into rice mixture and bake, covered, for 45 minutes at 350 degrees.

Preparation time: 1 1/2 hours   Yield: 6 servings

CHEESE GRITS

1 c. quick grits, without salt
1 stick butter
2 beaten eggs
1 (10 oz.) stick sharp cheese,
  grated

2 tsp. salt
1/2 tsp. onion salt
1/4 tsp. white pepper
1/4 tsp. garlic salt

Cook grits according to package directions. Add other ingredients and stir until cheese melts. Place in a deep baking dish and bake at 350 degrees for 1 hour.

Preparation time: 1 hour 15 minutes   Yield: 6 - 8 servings

ITALIAN RICE

1/2 c. melted butter
1/2 c. chopped onion
2 c. brown rice
4 c. beef bouillon

1/2 c. Parmesan cheese
1/2 c. chopped walnuts
1 1/2 tsp. salt

Sauté onion in melted butter until tender. Boil rice in 2 cups beef bouillon, covered, for 15 minutes. Combine all ingredients and place in casserole; cover and bake 1 hour at 350 degrees. Check occasionally and add boiling water if too dry.

Preparation time: 1 1/2 hours   Yield: 8 servings

EGGPLANT/SPINACH PARMESAN

1 large eggplant
1/4 c. butter
1/4 c. wheat germ
1 (10 oz.) pkg. chopped spinach
2 Tbsp. butter
2 Tbsp. whole wheat flour

1 c. milk
1/2 tsp. salt
1/8 tsp. pepper
1/8 tsp. nutmeg
1/4 c. slivered almonds
1/4 c. Parmesan cheese

Slice eggplant in 1/4 inch crosswise slices, dip in butter and cover with wheat germ. Broil for 3-5 minutes, until toasted and tender. Cook spinach in vegetable steamer; drain well. Meanwhile, melt 2 tablespoons butter in skillet. Combine flour, milk, and seasonings in blender. Blend until smooth, then pour into skillet; cook and stir until thickened. Add sauce and almonds to spinach, then top each eggplant slice with 1 - 2 tablespoons of spinach mixture. Top with Parmesan cheese and return to broiler for 2-3 minutes.

Preparation time: 30 minutes   Yield: 6 servings

SPICY CARROTS

2 (1 lb.) bags carrots, sliced
   and cooked
1 c. chopped onion
1/2 c. chopped green pepper
1 c. honey
3/4 c. cider vinegar

2 (6 oz.) cans tomato paste
1/2 c. safflower oil
1 tsp. mustard
Several dashes Tabasco sauce
Salt
Pepper

Prepare and cook carrots; drain and set aside. Combine other ingredients; stir well and season to taste with salt and pepper. Add carrots, cover and refrigerate several hours or overnight.

Preparation time: 30 minutes +   Yield: 12 servings
                standing time overnight

BAKED CARROTS AND LIMAS

2 c. sliced carrots
2 c. fresh lima beans
1 1/2 c. celery
1 1/2 c. fresh tomatoes
1/2 c. tomato puree

1/4 c. minced onion
Salt and pepper to taste
1/2 c. sharp cheese, grated
4 Tbsp. melted butter

Cook carrots and limas in vegetable steamer until tender. Drain and add celery, tomatoes, puree, onion, salt and pepper. Pour into buttered casserole dish and top with cheese, then drizzle butter over all. Bake, covered, at 350 degrees for 35-40 minutes.

Preparation time: 1 hour   Yield: 6 - 8 servings

PARSLEYED CARROTS

1 lb. carrots (baby carrots
   if possible)
2 Tbsp. butter
1 Tbsp. lemon juice

3/4 tsp. parsley
1/2 tsp. garlic salt
Dash white pepper

Cook carrots in steamer until tender, about 20 minutes. Drain water off and mix other ingredients in saucepan with carrots. Stir gently until butter melts.

Preparation time: 30 minutes   Yield: 4 servings

EGGPLANT PARMESAN

1 large eggplant
3 beaten eggs
1/2 c. whole wheat bread crumbs
1/2 c. wheat germ
3/4 c. safflower oil

1/2 c. grated Parmesan cheese
2 tsp. dried oregano
8 oz. sliced Mozzarella cheese
3 (8 oz.) cans tomato sauce

Peel eggplant; slice in 1/4 inch pieces. Mix whole wheat bread crumbs and wheat germ; dip eggplant slices first into egg, then into crumbs. Sauté in hot oil until golden on both sides. Layer eggplant, Parmesan and Mozzarella, then top with tomato sauce, to which oregano has been added. Repeat until all ingredients have been used, topping last layer with Mozzarella. Bake uncovered, at 350 degrees for 30 minutes.

Preparation time: 1 hour   Yield: 6 servings

GERMAN POTATO SALAD

4 c. crosswise sliced potatoes,
  peeling on
1 c. chopped onion
2 Tbsp. butter or margarine
1/4 c. apple cider vinegar
2 tsp. honey

1 3/4 tsp. salt
1/4 tsp. black pepper
1/2 c. mayonnaise*
1 Tbsp. parsley
2 Tbsp. bacon bits

Cook potatoes in vegetable steamer until tender, about 15 minutes. Meanwhile, brown onion in butter for 3-5 minutes, then stir in vinegar, honey, salt, pepper, mayonnaise and parsley. Place potatoes in a greased casserole dish, pour sauce over and stir to mix. Top with bacon bits and cover; bake at 400 degrees for 15 minutes.

Preparation time: 40 minutes   Yield: 6 - 8 servings

AMERICAN POTATO CASSEROLE

4 c. potatoes sliced crosswise
  with skin on
3/4 c. mayonnaise*
1 1/2 c. grated American cheese

1/4 c. chopped onion
1 tsp. salt
1/4 tsp. pepper
2 tsp. melted butter

Cook potatoes in vegetable steamer until tender, about 15 minutes. Combine mayonnaise, cheese, onion, salt and pepper. Place half of potatoes in a casserole dish, cover with half the cheese mixture; repeat with remaining potatoes and cheese. Drizzle melted butter over all. Bake covered, at 400 degrees for 10-15 minutes, until cheese melts.

Preparation time: 30 minutes   Yield: 6 servings

HOT POTATO SOUFFLÉ

6 eggs
1/2 c. heavy cream
1/4 tsp. celery seed
1/2 tsp. onion salt
3/4 - 1 tsp. salt

1/4 tsp. white pepper
Several dashes Tabasco sauce
1 c. cooked potato, cubed
1/2 onion in chunks
11 oz. cream cheese

Butter a 6 cup soufflé dish or 5-6 individual dishes. Place eggs, cream and seasonings in blender; whirl until smooth. Cut cream cheese in chunks and add with onion and potato while motor is running. Process until smooth; adjust seasoning if necessary. Pour into prepared dish and bake at 375 degrees for 45 (soft center), or 50 (firm center), minutes. Serve immediately

Preparation time: 1 hour   Yield: 6 servings

BAKED ONIONS

12 small onions (or 1 can
   Durkee's boiling onions)
1 Tbsp. unbleached flour
3/4 c. milk
1/2 tsp. salt

1/4 tsp. white pepper
1 c. grated Cheddar cheese
Cayenne pepper to taste (about
   1/8 tsp.)
1/4 c. roasted, salted sunflower seeds

Boil onions until tender, or if canned, drain well. Place in the bottom of a buttered 1 quart casserole. Melt butter in a small skillet, stir in flour. Add milk, stirring with a wire whisk until smooth. Cook and stir until thickened, about 1 minute. Add cheese and stir until melted; season with salt, pepper and cayenne. Pour over onions and top with sunflower seeds. Cover, bake at 400 degrees for 20 minutes or until bubbly.

Preparation time: 30 minutes   Yield: 4 servings

ASPARAGUS CASSEROLE

1 (10 oz.) pkg. asparagus pieces
3 eggs, hard-boiled
1 small can peas (or 1 c.
   frozen peas)
1 jar small cooked onions

4 oz. sharp cheese, grated
1/4 c. blanched, slivered almonds
1/3 c. mayonnaise*
Salt and pepper to taste
1/4 c. wheat germ

Cook asparagus in vegetable steamer; hard-boil eggs. Place asparagus in a large bowl; chop hard-boiled eggs and add to asparagus along with drained peas, drained onions, almonds, and cheese. Add mayonnaise and stir to mix; season to taste with salt and pepper. Place in a buttered 1 1/2 quart casserole and top with wheat germ. Bake uncovered at 375 degrees for 25-30 minutes or better still, microwave on high for 10 minutes.

Preparation time: 30-45 minutes   Yield: 6 servings

FRESH BROCCOLI CASSEROLE

1 bunch fresh broccoli
2 Tbsp. butter or margarine
1/4 c. onion
1 c. sour cream
2 tsp. honey

1 tsp. cider vinegar
1/2 tsp. paprika
1/2 tsp. salt
1/2 c. natural raw cashews, chopped

Wash broccoli and separate into flowers with 3-4 inches of stem. Steam in vegetable steamer for 5-6 minutes. Sauté onion in butter; remove from heat. Add sour cream, honey, vinegar, paprika and salt. Combine cooked broccoli with sour cream sauce, stirring carefully so that flowers will not be torn. Top with cashews; serve.

Preparation time: 15 minutes   Yield: 6 servings

SPANISH RICE

1 1/2 c. raw brown rice
1 1/2 c. tomato juice
2 1/2 c. beef broth
1/2 c. butter or margarine

1 c. chopped onion
1/2 c. chopped green pepper
1 1/2 tsp. salt
1 can water chestnuts, sliced

Combine all ingredients and bring to a boil; simmer, covered, for 15 minutes. Turn into a greased casserole and bake, covered, at 350 degrees for 1 hour.

Preparation time: 1 hour 20 minutes   Yield: 8 servings

ZUCCHINI IN SOUR CREAM

4 c. sliced, unpeeled zucchini
1 c. sour cream
1/4 c. milk

1 c. chopped onion
1 tsp. salt
1 c. sharp Cheddar cheese, grated

Steam zucchini in vegetable steamer for 3 minutes only; turn into buttered casserole. Combine sour cream, milk, onion and salt; pour over zucchini and stir gently. Top with cheese and bake at 400 degrees for 15 minutes, or microwave on high for 5 minutes.

Preparation time: 30 minutes   Yield: 6 - 8 servings

ZUCCHINI AND POTATO SCRAMBLE

2 Tbsp. butter or margarine
1/2 c. chopped onion
2 medium zucchini, sliced,
  unpeeled
2 medium potatoes, cubed,
  unpeeled

2 large unpeeled tomatoes,
  cut in fourths
Salt
Pepper
Parmesan cheese

Sauté onion in butter; add vegetables. Cover and cook on low until tender, about 20 minutes. Add water as necessary to prevent sticking; season with plenty of salt, pepper and Parmesan. Serve piping hot.

Preparation time: 30 minutes   Yield: 4 servings

MAIN DISHES

CHEESY BAKED EGGS WITH SPINACH

4 eggs
8 slices (1/2 oz. each) American
  cheese
1 (10 oz.) pkg. frozen, chopped
  spinach, cooked and salted according to package directions

4 Tbsp. grated onion
4 Tbsp. butter
Salt to taste
Pepper to taste

In each of 4 individual casserole dishes, melt 1 tablespoon butter. Place 1 slice of cheese in each one, and top with 1/4 cup cooked spinach. Follow with another slice of cheese, then break an egg to top each one. Salt and pepper the egg to taste, and bake at 350 degrees for 10-12 minutes.

Preparation time: 25 minutes   Yield: 4 servings

Hint: I usually cook the spinach and grate the onions the night before serving; then it can be popped in the microwave for 3 minutes.

Preparation time: 5 minutes

BAKED EGGS WITH CHICKEN LIVERS

8 eggs
1 lb. chicken livers
1/4 c. butter
1/2 c. onion

1 Tbsp. dried parsley
1/4 c. evaporated milk
Salt to taste
Pepper to taste

Sauté onion in butter for a few minutes, then add chicken livers and saute for 10 minutes. Beat the eggs together with the seasonings and add to the livers. Turn into 4 buttered individual casserole dishes and bake for 20-25 minutes at 325 degrees.

Preparation time: 40 minutes   Yield: 4 servings

BLACK-EYED SUSAN EGGS

2 Tbsp. butter
2 diced green onions or
  1 c. chopped onion
6 large chopped black olives

2oz. Provolone cheese, finely diced
2 tsp. grated Parmesan cheese
4 beaten eggs
Salt and pepper to taste

Sauté onions in butter until softened. Add other ingredients to eggs and pour into skillet. Stir over low heat until eggs are set; cheese will melt and make eggs creamy. Serve at once.

Preparation time: 12-15 minutes   Yield: 4 servings

EGGS & MUSHROOMS

4 Tbsp. butter
1 c. sliced fresh mushrooms
1/4 c. diced onions
1/4 c. diced green pepper

3 eggs
2 Tbsp. milk
Salt to taste
Pepper to taste

Melt butter; sauté mushrooms, onions and peppers until tender, about 5 minutes. Whip eggs with milk until light; stir into mushroom mixture and cook over low heat until set. Season with salt and pepper and serve immediately.

Preparation time: 10 minutes   Yield: 2 servings

EGGS MORNAY

2 Tbsp. butter or margarine
2 Tbsp. whole wheat flour
1 c. milk
1/4 tsp. salt
Dash pepper and nutmeg

1/4 c. grated Swiss cheese
1/4 c. grated Parmesan cheese
6 eggs
6 whole wheat rusks or biscuits

Melt butter; stir in flour. Add milk and cook, stirring until thickened. Stir in seasonings and cheeses; blend until cheeses melt. Poach 6 eggs; top each rusk with an egg and a generous spoonful of Mornay sauce. Serve at once.

Preparation time: 10 minutes   Yield: 6 servings

CHEESE CUSTARD

1 c. evaporated milk
1 1/4 c. sharp Cheddar cheese,
  grated
4 eggs

1/2 tsp. salt
1/4 tsp. white pepper
Dash cayenne

Beat all ingredients well; pour into 1 quart baking dish. Set in a pan of water and bake uncovered, at 350 degrees, 45-55 minutes, until done, (or bake in microwave on high 15 minutes).

Preparation time: 1 hour   Yield: 4 servings

ROQUEFORT CHEESE SOUFFLÉ

6 eggs
1/2 c. heavy cream
1/4 tsp. pepper
1/4 - 1/2 tsp. salt

Several dashes Tabasco sauce
4 oz. Blue or Roquefort cheese
11 oz. cream cheese
1 Tbsp. minced dried onion

Place eggs, cream and seasonings in blender; whirl until smooth. Cut cheeses into chunks and add while motor is running. Add onion and pour into a buttered 5 cup soufflé dish or 6 buttered individual dishes. Bake at 375 degrees for 45 (soft center) or 50 (firm center) minutes. Serve immediately.

Preparation time: 55 minutes   Yield: 6 servings
      Hint: Bake individual dishes for 15-20 minutes.

CHEDDAR CHEESE SOUFFLÉ

6 eggs
1/2 c. heavy cream
1/4 c. Parmesan cheese
1/2 tsp. mustard
1/2 tsp. salt

1/4 tsp. pepper
1/2 lb. sharp Cheddar cheese
11 oz. cream cheese
Tabasco sauce to taste

Butter a 5 cup soufflé dish or 5-6 individual soufflé dishes. Place eggs, cream, Parmesan cheese, mustard, salt and pepper in blender. Whirl until smooth. Cut cheeses into cubes and add through lid to blender while motor is running. When all the cheese has been added, whirl at high speed for 5 seconds. Add Tabasco sauce as desired; mix well. Pour into soufflé dish and bake at 375 degrees for 45 (soft center), or 50 (firm center) minutes. Serve immediately.

Preparation time: 55-60 minutes   Yield: 6 servings
      Hint: Can be prepared and held at room temperature for 1-2 hours, or refrigerated for 24 hours and cooked 10 minutes longer.

CHEESE SOUFFLÉ (traditional)
Reprinted from the Starr Cookbook
by permission of WATE-TV, Knoxville, Tn.

4 Tbsp. melted butter
4 Tbsp. flour (unbleached)
1 1/2 c. hot milk
1 tsp. salt

Cayenne to taste
8 oz. grated sharp cheese
6 eggs, room temperature,
separated

Blend flour with melted butter. Add hot milk gradually, stirring constantly. Add seasonings; cook until smooth and creamy, stirring constantly. Remove from heat and stir in cheese, stirring until cheese melts. Add well beaten egg yolks, mixing thoroughly. Then add stiffly beaten egg whites, folding carefully. Turn into well buttered 2 quart soufflé dish and bake at 300 degrees for 1 hour. Serve immediately.

Preparation time: 1 1/2 hours   Yield: 6 - 8 servings

BAKED OATMEAL

1 c. oats (not quick-cooked)
2 c. water
2 eggs, room temperature
2 Tbsp. butter or margarine

1/4 c. honey
1/2 tsp. salt
1 tsp. lemon rind
1/3 c. raisins or dates

Place oats and water in a medium saucepan; bring to a boil. Reduce heat to low and cook 5 minutes, stirring often. Remove from heat. Add butter or margarine, salt, honey, raisins and lemon rind; stir to mix. Separate eggs; add yolks to oatmeal mixture and beat whites until stiff peaks form. Fold in whites and turn into 1 5-cup soufflé type dish or 4 individual casserole dishes, well greased. Bake at 400 degrees for 15 minutes. Serve immediately.

Preparation time: 25 minutes   Yield: 4 servings

FRENCH ONION SOUP

6 c. beef stock (may use
   Swanson brand)
6 medium onions
Salt and pepper to taste

6 Tbsp. butter (no substitute)
6 slices dilly bread*, buttered
   and toasted
Parmesan cheese

Brown onions, sliced thin in butter, over low heat until tender. Add beef stock and simmer 15 minutes. Season to taste; pour into individual casserole or soup dishes. Cut dilly bread, toasted and buttered, into small chunks. Place in soup, sprinkle on Parmesan cheese. Broil for a minute, until cheese melts. Serve piping hot.

Preparation time: 30 minutes   Yield: 4 - 6 servings

MINESTRONE SOUP

1/4 c. safflower oil
2 chopped medium onions,
  about 2 c.
1/4 tsp. garlic powder
1 c. each: carrots and celery
1 (28-oz) can tomatoes with juice
4 tsp. salt
1/4 tsp. white pepper
1/4 tsp. cayenne pepper

1/2 c. whole wheat macaroni,
  uncooked
1 c. fresh green beans,
  diagonally cut
2 medium zucchini, sliced
2 c. washed, fresh spinach leaves,
  stems discarded
2 (15-oz.) cans navy beans
Parmesan cheese

Sauté onion in safflower oil; add garlic. Add carrots, celery, tomatoes, salt, white pepper, cayenne and 4 cups water. Bring to a boil, then simmer 40 minutes. Add green beans, macaroni, zucchini, spinach and navy beans. Bring to a boil, then simmer for 30 minutes more. Serve topped with a generous sprinkling of Parmesan cheese.

Preparation time: 1 1/2 hours   Yield: 2 1/2 quarts soup

COUNTRY-STYLE PEA SOUP

1 pkg. split green peas,
  1 lb. size
8 c. water
4 c. tomato juice
2 c. fresh, diced pork
1 1/2 c. chopped potatoes,
  skin on

1 c. chopped celery
1 c. chopped onion
1 c. chopped carrots
1 bay leaf
1 tsp. salt
1/4 tsp. pepper
Few drops Tabasco sauce

Brown pork well in saucepan. Meanwhile, mix other ingredients together and bring to a boil. Add browned pork and simmer 1 1/2 - 2 hours. Serve piping hot.

Preparation time: 2 hours   Yield: 10 - 12 servings

CHEDDAR CHOWDER

1/2 stick butter or margarine	3 c. milk
1 onion, peeled and chopped	1 tsp. salt
1/2 c. chopped celery	1/4 tsp. white pepper
1/2 c. chopped carrots	1/2 tsp. chili powder
3 Tbsp. unbleached flour	Several drops Tabasco sauce
1 c. chicken broth	8 oz. grated sharp Cheddar cheese

Melt butter, add onions, carrots and celery. Cook over low heat, covered, for 10 minutes. Place in blender and whirl until smooth. Return to pan. Add flour to onion mixture, cook and stir over medium heat until it bubbles and thickens. Add broth and milk; add seasonings. Stir with wire whip and simmer 5 minutes. Remove from heat; stir in cheese, continuing to stir, until melted.

Preparation time: 30 minutes   Yield: 4 servings

FISH CHOWDER

1 lb. frozen flounder or other fish	1/2 c. chopped onion
2 1/2 c. cubed potatoes, skins on	2 c. evaporated milk
4 slices salt-cured or fresh hickory-smoked bacon	3 Tbsp. unbleached flour

Thaw fish, cut into small cubes, checking carefully for bones. Cook bacon until crisp; drain. Brown onion in bacon grease. Measure 2 cups water into saucepan. Cook potatoes 5 minutes, then add fish and cook 10 minutes. While potatoes and fish are cooking, measure milk and flour into blender. Whirl until smooth. Add milk mixture and bacon-onion mixture to fish and potatoes. Cook and stir over medium heat until thickened. Adjust seasonings with salt and pepper.

Preparation time: 30 minutes   Yield: 4 servings

CREAM OF POTATO SOUP

4 Tbsp. butter
1/2 c. diced onion
1/3 c. unbleached flour
2 c. beef broth

2 c. half & half or evaporated milk
Lots of salt and pepper to taste
4 c. diced potatoes, cooked with
  skins on

Cook potatoes; set aside. Melt butter in 2 quart saucepan; sauté onion until tender. Blend in flour, then beef broth. Stir vigorously with wire whip; cook and stir over medium heat until thickened. Add cream and potatoes and season to taste with salt and lots of pepper. Serve piping hot.

Preparation time: 30 minutes   Yield: 4 - 5 servings

CREAM OF CHICKEN SOUP

1 c. cooked, cubed chicken
2 Tbsp. chopped onion
2 Tbsp. butter
3 Tbsp. unbleached flour
2 c. chicken broth

1 c. evaporated milk
1/4 tsp. salt
1 Tbsp. lemon juice
1/8 tsp. cayenne

Make a cream sauce of butter, flour and chicken broth, stirring constantly until bubbly and thickened. Add chicken, milk and seasonings and heat throughout.

Preparation time: 15 minutes   Yield: 4 - 6 servings

CREAM OF MUSHROOM SOUP

3 c. sliced, fresh mushrooms
1/3 c. onion, diced
6 Tbsp. butter, (no substitute)
7 Tbsp. unbleached flour
1 1/2 tsp. salt

3/4 tsp. nutmeg
1/2 tsp. white pepper
3 c. chicken broth
1 1/2 c. half & half

Wash mushrooms; remove stems and slice thin. Sauté mushrooms and onions over medium heat for a few minutes, until mushrooms are browned and onion is tender. Blend in flour and seasonings, add chicken broth and stir with wooden spoon until thick and bubbly. Add cream and heat again if necessary. Serve at once.

Preparation time: 20 minutes   Yield: 1 1/2 quarts soup or
                                              4 - 6 servings

Hint: I like to make this recipe in multiple amounts, storing some in 1 cup containers in refrigerator for recipe use within a day or two.

FISH & CHIPS

4 medium baking potatoes,
  scrubbed
1 c. safflower oil

1/2 c. raw wheat germ
1/2 tsp. salt
1 lb. fish fillets

Slice potatoes into large French-fry shapes, keeping peeling on. Bake in a 350 degree oven for 15 minutes or microwave on high for 3-4 minutes. Fry in hot safflower oil until tender and browned well. about 4 minutes. Drain and salt; remove to warm platter. Coat fish in wheat germ and salt mixture and fry in remaining safflower oil until golden and tender, about 3-4 minutes. Serve with potatoes on warmed platter.

Preparation time: 30 minutes   Yield: 4 servings

SECOND-HELPING HADDOCK

1 lb. frozen haddock fillets
4 Tbsp. butter or margarine
1/2 c. chopped onion
1 egg, beaten
1/4 c. milk
1 Tbsp. parsley

1/2 tsp. salt
1/8 tsp. pepper
1/2 c. bread crumbs (from
  homemade bread)
1/2 c. grated sharp cheese

Thaw haddock; bake uncovered for 10 minutes at 350 degrees (or microwave on high for 4 minutes). Meanwhile, sauté onion in butter and combine with egg, milk, parsley, salt and pepper. Add bread crumbs. Remove fish from oven and break up with fork into small pieces. Add milk mixture and stir well. Return to casserole and top with cheese; bake 10 minutes more at 350 degrees (or microwave 3-4 minutes; until cheese melts).

Preparation time: 30 minutes   Yield: 4 servings

FILLET OF SOLE WITH GREEN GRAPES
(mild and creamy)

1 (1-lb.) pkg. fillet of sole, thawed
4 Tbsp. butter or margarine
2 shallots, chopped fine
1 c. chicken broth

Salt and pepper
4 Tbsp. heavy cream
1 Tbsp. whole wheat flour
1 1/2 c. seedless green grapes

Separate fillets; rinse and drain on paper towels. Melt butter and sauté shallots; add fish fillets and broth. Cover and cook on low heat for 10 minutes. Remove to heat proof serving platter. Combine cream and whole wheat flour; whisk or blend until smooth. Pour over fillets and arrange grapes around fillets. Broil for 3-5 minutes, until lightly brown (watch carefully!). Serve piping hot.

Preparation time: 25 minutes   Yield: 4 servings

BAKED STUFFED FLOUNDER

1 lb. frozen flounder fillets,
   thawed
2 Tbsp. butter or margarine
1/4 c. chopped green pepper
1/4 c. chopped onion

1/2 c. (homemade) bread crumbs
2 eggs, beaten
1/2 tsp. salt
1/4 tsp. pepper
1/2 c. butter or margarine

Separate fillets, rinse and drain on paper towels. Melt 2 tablespoons butter in small skillet; sauté pepper and onion until tender. Remove from heat, stir in bread crumbs and eggs, salt and pepper. Place 2 tablespoons stuffing in the center of each flounder fillet; roll up and place in a buttered casserole dish, seam down. Top with remaining stuffing and drizzle with melted butter. Bake 20-25 minutes at 350 degrees.

Preparation time: 40 minutes   Yield: 4 servings

SAVORY BAKED PERCH

1 lb. frozen perch fillet (or
   other desired fish), thawed

3 Tbsp. butter or margarine
1/2 c. crunchy casserole topping*

Melt butter in bottom of a rectangular baking dish; coat fish in butter then top with crunchy topping. Bake at 375 degrees for 25 minutes.

Preparation time: 30 minutes   Yield: 4 servings

CRAB STUFFED POTATOES
Reprinted from the Starr Cookbook
by permission of WATE-TV, Knoxville, Tn.

4 baking potatoes
1/2 c. butter (no substitute)
1/2 c. light cream
1 tsp. salt

4 Tbsp. grated onion
1 c. sharp cheese
1 can crabmeat
Tabasco sauce and pepper to taste

Bake potatoes at 350 degrees for 1 1/4 hours or until tender. Cut in half lengthwise, scoop out potato and whip with above ingredients. Refill shells and reheat at 425 degrees for 15 minutes. These freeze nicely.

Preparation time: 2 hours

Yield: 4 - 6 servings

SEAFOOD CASSEROLE

1/2 c. butter (no substitute)
1/2 c. unbleached flour
4 c. evaporated milk
2 tsp. salt
3 c. sharp cheese, grated
1/4 tsp. pepper

1/4 tsp. red pepper
1/2 tsp. dry mustard
1 lb. cooked shrimp
3 cans crabmeat
Tabasco sauce to taste
1 (10-oz.) bag peas, cooked

Melt butter; stir in flour; cook until bubbly and gradually add milk, stirring until smooth. Add salt and grated cheese; cook and stir until cheese has melted and mixture is thick. Add seasonings, seafood and peas and heat through. Serve over toast points.

Preparation time: 40 minutes

Yield: 10 - 12 servings

SPAGHETTI SHRIMP

1 lb. cooked shrimp
2 (15 oz) cans tomato sauce
1 c. chopped onion
1 tsp. oregano
1 1/2 tsp. basil
1/2 tsp. garlic chips

2 Tbsp. honey
1 tsp. salt
1/2 tsp. pepper
1 (5 oz.) pkg. Romano cheese, grated
1/2 c. Parmesan cheese
8 oz. whole wheat spaghetti

Combine tomato sauce, onions, and seasonings. Simmer, uncovered, 30 minutes. Add shrimp and simmer until sauce thickens and flavors mix well, about 30 minutes. Add cheeses and stir over very low heat until melted. Serve over spaghetti.

Preparation time: 1 hour

Yield: 4 servings

CRAB PARMESAN

2 Tbsp. chopped onion
2 Tbsp. chopped green pepper
1/4 c. butter or margarine
1/4 c. whole wheat flour
1 1/3 c. milk
1 Tbsp. chives
1 Tbsp. parsley
1 Tbsp. prepared mustard
1/8 tsp. cayenne

Few drops of Tabasco sauce
1/2 tsp. paprika
1/3 c. Parmesan cheese
1 tsp. salt
2 eggs
2 (6 1/2 oz. size) cans crabmeat
2 Tbsp. melted butter
Additional Parmesan

Sauté onion and pepper in butter until tender. Place flour and milk in the blender and process until smooth; pour all at once into butter mixture. Cook and stir over medium heat until sauce has thickened, about 2 minutes. Remove from heat and stir in chives, parsley, mustard, cayenne, Tabasco sauce, paprika, Parmesan and salt. Beat eggs with fork and add to creamed sauce along with drained crabmeat. Mix well and pour into 1 1/2 quart casserole. Top with melted butter and additional Parmesan. Bake at 350 degrees for 30 minutes, or microwave on high for 10 minutes.

Preparation time: 45 minutes   Yield: 6 servings

CHICKEN & WILD RICE CASSEROLE

1 c. uncooked wild rice
2 Tbsp. butter
1/2 tsp. salt
1/4 c. butter
1/4 c. unbleached flour
1 c. fresh mushroom caps,
   sliced thin
1 c. chopped onions

2 c. half & half
Salt and pepper to taste
Cayenne to taste
3 c. cooked, cubed chicken
2 Tbsp. dried parsley
1 c. water
1/2 c. sunflower seeds

Cook wild rice in 2 3/4 cups water with butter and salt until water is absorbed. Meanwhile, melt butter; sauté mushrooms and onions until tender, about 5 minutes. Blend in flour, then cream. Stir constantly with wire whisk until thickened. Season with salt, pepper and cayenne to taste, then blend into chicken. Add parsley, rice, and 1 cup water; turn into buttered 2 quart casserole and top with sunflower seeds. Bake 30 minutes at 350 degrees.

Preparation time: 1 hour   Yield: 8 servings

BARBECUED CHICKEN

1 can tomato puree
3 Tbsp. vinegar
1 Tbsp. minced onion
2 Tbsp. honey
1 tsp. chili powder
1 tsp. garlic salt
1 tsp. salt

1 tsp. paprika
1 tsp. dry mustard
1/2 tsp. pepper
1/2 tsp. cinnamon
1/2 c. water
10 - 12 chicken thighs or other
    pieces

Mix all ingredients and pour over chicken. Bake at 325 degrees for 2 hours, uncovered. Baste occasionally.

Preparation time: 2 hours 15 minutes   Yield: 6 - 8 servings

CHICKEN SPAGHETTI

1/4 c. butter or margarine
1/4 c. onion
1 c. sliced fresh mushrooms
2 Tbsp. flour
2 c. chicken broth
1 Tbsp. lemon juice
1 tsp. salt to taste
1/4 tsp. pepper

3 c. chopped chicken
1 c. chopped celery
3 pimentoes, chopped
1 1/2 c. mushroom soup
1 (8 oz.) pkg. whole wheat
    spaghetti, cooked
1 c. shredded Cheddar cheese

Sauté onion and mushrooms in butter for 5 minutes. Stir in flour, then chicken broth. Cook and stir until slightly thickened. Add other ingredients except cheese; turn into casserole dish and top with cheese. Bake at 350 degrees for 30-40 minutes, covered.

Preparation time: 1 hour   Yield: 8 servings

CHICKEN ROLLUPS
Recipe from Good Housekeeping

1/3 c. chopped, salted peanuts	1/2 c. butter
1/4 c. minced parsley	1/2 tsp. paprika
1/2 tsp. salt	1 tsp. salt
6 whole chicken breasts or	1 1/4 c. milk
12 boned halves	2 tsp. prepared mustard

Bone chicken breasts; pound to 1/4 inch thickness. Stuff with mixture of peanuts, parsley and 1/2 teaspoon salt; secure with toothpicks. Melt butter in 13 X 9 inch baking pan, add paprika and 1 teaspoon salt and mix well. Place chicken rolls in butter and turn to coat well. Bake for 45-50 minutes, uncovered, at 400 degrees. Baske occasionally. Remove chicken from oven, pour off drippings. Measure 3 tablespoons drippings and blend with 2 tablespoons flour, 1/2 teaspoon salt and mustard. Cook and stir until bubbly, add milk and cook until thickened. Cover seasoning with salt and pepper if needed; pour over chicken and serve.

Preparation time: 1 1/4 hours   Yield: 6 - 8 servings

CHICKEN IMPERIAL

1 frying chicken, cut up	2 Tbsp. dried parsley
1/2 c. melted butter	1 tsp. salt
2/3 c. wheat germ	1/4 tsp. white pepper
2/3 c. Parmesan cheese	1/4 tsp. garlic powder

Wash chicken and pat dry. Mix wheat germ, cheese and seasonings. Roll chicken pieces in this mixture, place in pan and drizzle with melted butter. Bake, covered, at 350 degrees for 30 minutes; uncover and bake 30 more minutes or until chicken is tender.

Preparation time: 1 hour 10 minutes   Yield: 4 - 6 servings

CHICKEN SUPREME

2 c. dairy sour cream
1/4 c. lemon juice
1/4 tsp. Tabasco sauce
2 tsp. celery salt
2 tsp. paprika
6 whole chicken breasts, boned

2 tsp. salt
1/2 tsp. pepper
1 3/4 c. whole wheat bread crumbs
1/4 c. butter
1/2 c. shortening

Early in day, combine sour cream with lemon juice and all the spices. Add the 6 chicken breasts, coating each piece well. Cover, let stand in refrigerator until 1 1/2 hours before serving. Preheat oven to 350 degrees. Combine crumbs with salt and pepper; roll coated chicken in crumbs. Sauté until light golden; bake uncovered for 50-60 minutes.

Preparation time: 1 day   Yield: 6 - 8 servings

DEVILED CHICKEN
Reprinted from the Starr Cookbook
by permission of WATE-TV, Knoxville, Tn.

14 - 16 chicken thighs
1 c. unbleached flour
1 tsp. paprika
1 tsp. salt
1/4 tsp. pepper

1/2 c. butter or margarine
2 tsp. prepared mustard
1 Tbsp. instant onion
1/2 tsp. salt
2 c. chicken broth

Wash chicken thighs; mix flour, paprika, salt and pepper and coat chicken in mixture. Brown in butter on both sides until golden and place in casserole dish. Stir 2 tablespoons flour mixture into remaining butter; add mustard, onion, salt and broth. Stir until thick and bubbly, then pour over chicken. Cover and bake 40-45 minutes at 350 degrees.

Preparation time: 1 hour   Yield: 6 - 8 servings

CHICKEN PARMESAN ROLLS

4 whole chicken breasts,
  or 8 halves, boned
4 Tbsp. butter
1/3 c. whole wheat flour
1/3 c. Parmesan cheese
1/2 tsp. paprika

1/2 tsp. salt
1/4 tsp. pepper
1/2 c. milk
1 egg
1/4 c. butter, melted

Divide 4 tablespoons butter into 8 pieces; roll up tightly inside boned chicken breasts which have been pounded to 1/4 inch thickness. Secure tightly with toothpicks. Combine flour, cheese, paprika, salt and pepper in one bowl; milk and egg in another bowl. Dip chicken rolls into flour mixture, then into milk and back into flour mixture. Place in a casserole dish and drizzle with melted butter. Bake, covered, at 350 degrees for 1 hour, (or microwave on "high" for 15 minutes), allowing to stand a few minutes before serving. Remove toothpicks.

Preparation time: 1 hour 15 minutes   Yield: 4 - 6 servings

CHICKEN DIVAN

3 c. cooked cubed chicken
2 (8 oz.) pkg. cream cheese
2 boxes frozen, chopped
  broccoli

3/4 c. Parmesan cheese
2 1/2 c. milk
3/4 tsp. garlic salt
1 tsp. salt

Cook broccoli until tender; drain. Melt cream cheese in top of double boiler; add salts, milk and Parmesan cheese. Stir until creamy. Layer half the cream sauce with broccoli, then chicken and remaining cream sauce. Bake 30 minutes at 350 degrees.

Preparation time: 1 hour   Yield: 8 - 10 servings

CHICKEN BREASTS WITH SWEET POTATO RICE
Reprinted from the Starr Cookbook
by permission of WATE-TV, Knoxville, Tn.

8 boned chicken breasts
2 c. cream of chicken soup*
2 egg yolks, beaten
1/4 tsp. dill weed
1/8 tsp. nutmeg
1/4 tsp. salt

1/4 tsp. pepper
1 c. cubed sweet potato
1/4 c. orange juice
1/3 c. water
1 c. brown rice
1 Tbsp. butter

Boil rice until partially done. Mix with sweet potato, orange juice, water and butter. Place in casserole, topping with uncooked chicken breasts. Cover with soup, egg yolks, and seasonings. Bake, covered, at 275 degrees for 2 1/2 hours or until chicken is tender.

Preparation time: 3 hours   Yield: 4 - 6 servings

CREAMED CHICKEN LIVERS

1 lb. chicken livers
1 c. whole wheat flour
1 tsp. salt
1/2 tsp. pepper
2 slices salt pork or fresh bacon
1/4 c. butter or margarine

1 chopped onion
1 c. fresh mushrooms
2 Tbsp. butter or margarine
2 Tbsp. whole wheat flour
1 c. light cream
Salt, pepper, and a sprinkling
  of nutmeg

Shake chicken livers in a paper bag with flour, salt and pepper. Brown salt pork or bacon; remove and discard. Brown livers; remove; add 1/4 cup butter. Sauté onions and mushrooms for 3 to 4 minutes. Add 2 tablespoons butter and return livers to skillet. Reduce heat, cover, and cook for 5 minutes on medium heat. Combine cream and whole wheat flour; whirl in blender or mix with wire whisk until smooth. Pour into liver mixture and cook, stirring constantly, until thickened. Sprinkle with nutmeg and season to taste with salt and pepper. Serve over rusks or biscuits if desired.

Preparation time: 20 minutes   Yield: 4 servings

MEATY CORN BREAD

3 Tbsp. butter or margarine
1 c. onions, diced
1 c. green pepper, chopped
2 lb. ground chuck

1 (15 oz.) can tomato sauce
3 tsp. chili powder
2 tsp. salt
1/2 tsp. pepper

Brown onion, pepper and meat in butter. Add seasonings and tomato sauce. Simmer 15 minutes, then place in a 9 X 13 inch baking dish. Top with corn bread batter made from:

2 c. yellow corn meal
1/2 tsp. soda
2 beaten eggs
1 c. plain yogurt

1/4 c. water
1 tsp. baking powder
1 tsp. salt
6 Tbsp. melted butter

Add liquids to dry ingredients; stir until moistened. Spread over meat mixture and bake at 425 degrees for 25 minutes.

Preparation time: 1 hour   Yield: 6 - 8 servings

BEEF STROGANOFF

1/2 c. butter or margarine
2 onions, sliced thin
1 c. sliced, fresh mushrooms
3 lb. cubed, boneless sirloin
   roast
1 1/2 c. mushroom soup*

Salt and pepper to taste
1 c. sour cream
2 Tbsp. parsley
Buttered, cooked whole wheat
   noodles

Melt butter, sauté onions and mushrooms 5 minutes. Add meat and stir to brown. Add soup, salt and pepper and cover; cook 1 1/2 hours on low heat until tender. Just before serving, stir in sour cream and sprinkle with parsley. Serve on a bed of noodles.

Preparation time: 2 hours   Yield: 6 - 8 servings

BEEF STUFFED BUTTERNUT SQUASH

4 medium butternut squash
1/4 c. butter, melted
1/4 c. honey
4 c. cubed beef roast
  (sirloin is best)
2 Tbsp. butter
2 onions, sliced thin

1/4 c. water
1/4 c. honey
1/2 c. apple cider vinegar
1/3 c. tangy catsup*
1/2 c. raisins
1 1/2 tsp. salt
1/4 tsp. pepper

Halve squash lengthwise and remove seeds. Combine melted butter and honey; pour into large oblong casserole. Place squash, cut side down, in butter and honey mixture, cover, and bake at 325 degrees for 1 1/2 hours. Meanwhile, brown meat in 2 tablespoons butter. Add onions and water, cover, and simmer while preparing sauce. Combine honey, vinegar, catsup, raisins, salt and pepper and pour over meat. Cover and cook on low heat, adding water if necessary, until squash is done. To serve, fill cavity of squash with meat; pass extra meat.

Preparation time: 1 3/4 hours   Yield: 8 servings

FRIED STEAK WITH CREAM GRAVY

2 lb. top round or Parker House
  steak, cut into 4 serving pieces
6 Tbsp. butter
1/2 c. whole wheat flour

1/2 tsp. salt
1/4 tsp. pepper
1 c. light cream
2 Tbsp. whole wheat flour

Melt butter; coat steak in flour, salt and pepper mixture. Brown in butter on both sides; cover, reduce heat and cook very slowly 45 minutes. Remove steak to serving platter. Pour off excess grease, reserving 2 table-spoons. Combine light cream and 2 tablespoons whole wheat flour. Blend in blender or mix with wire whisk until smooth. Pour into pan and cook, stirring constantly, until gravy has thickened. Adjust taste with salt and pepper if necessary; pour over steak and serve immediately.

Preparation time: 1 hour   Yield: 4 servings

TASTY CREAMED LIVER

4 Tbsp. butter or margarine
1 c. diced onion
1 c. sliced, fresh mushrooms
1/4 c. whole wheat flour
1 1/2 c. light cream

1/2 tsp. salt
1/4 tsp. pepper
Dash of nutmeg
1 1/2 lb. calve's liver
1/2 c. whole wheat flour

Melt butter; sauté onion and mushrooms 5 minutes. Stir in flour, add cream, salt and pepper and cook, stirring constantly, until thickened. Coat liver in whole wheat flour, place in the bottom of a slow cooking ceramic pot. Pour mushroom sauce over, cover and cook on low 6-8 hours (or place in a casserole and bake at 325 degrees for 1 1/2 hours).

Preparation time: 6 - 8 hours   Yield: 4 servings

MARINATED STEAK AND MUSHROOM KABOBS
(delicious grilled outside)

1 1/2 c. safflower oil
1 c. honey
1 c. apple cider vinegar
1 c. tomato juice
1/3 c. dried onion
1/4 c. tangy catsup*
1/4 c. mustard

1 tsp. garlic salt
1/2 tsp. dried garlic chips
1/4 tsp. pepper
3 lb. sirloin tip roast,
   cut in 2 inch cubes
1/2 lb. fresh mushroom caps

Combine all ingredients except steak and mushrooms and stir well. Pour over cubed steak and washed mushroom caps; cover and marinate overnight. To cook, alternate steak and mushrooms on skewers and broil 6 inches from heat for 8-10 minutes, turning once and basting several times. Serve over rice (Italian Rice* is especially good).

Preparation time: 20 minutes +   Yield: 6 - 8 servings
                  overnight
    Hint: Save marinate to use again.

CAJUN COUNTRY MEAT LOAF

3 lb. lean ground beef
1 lb. ground pork
1 large onion, chopped fine

2 (8 oz.) can tomato sauce
1 c. wheat germ
1/4 tsp. salt

Mix thoroughly; make into 2 loaves and bake at 350 degrees for 1 hour 15 minutes. Top with sauce:

1/4 c. butter or margarine
1 c. sliced onions
1/2 c. chopped green pepper
2 Tbsp. honey
1/4 tsp. salt

1/4 tsp. pepper
1 large can whole tomatoes
1/4 c. whole wheat flour
1/2 c. water

Melt butter, add onion, pepper, honey, salt and pepper with juice from tomatoes. Simmer covered, 30 minutes. Stir flour into water, add to mixture with tomatoes. Cook until thickened, pour over meat loaf.

Preparation time: 1 1/2 hours   Yield: 8 servings

POT ROAST WITH SOUR CREAM GRAVY

2 Tbsp. butter or maragrine
1 (3-4 lb.) roast
2 onions, sliced
2 bay leaves
1 tsp. salt
1/4 tsp. pepper

2 c. water
1/4 c. oat or other whole
  grain flour
1 c. sour cream
1/2 tsp. mace
Salt and pepper to taste

Brown roast on all sides in butter; add onions, bay leaves, salt, pepper and water. Cover and bring to a boil; reduce heat and simmer 2 1/2 hours, until tender. Skim off any fat, remove roast from pan to serving platter. Thicken 1 cup of beef broth by putting 1/4 cup oat or other whole grain flour in blender with sour cream and mace. Mix well; pour into saucepan. Cook and stir until thickened, adjust seasonings if necessary, and pour over meat.

Preparation time: 3 hours   Yield: 6 servings

BEEF STEW WITH WHOLE WHEAT DUMPLINGS

2 lb. cubed stewing beef
2 Tbsp. safflower oil
4 c. hot water
2 sliced onions
2 bay leaves
1 Tbsp. salt
1/4 tsp. pepper

2 c. carrots, cut in 1 inch pieces
2 c. unpeeled, cubed potatoes
1 c. chopped celery
1 (10 oz.) pkg. frozen peas
1/4 c. whole wheat flour
1/2 c. cold water

Brown beef in oil; add water, onions, salt and pepper. Cover and simmer 2 hours. Add carrots and potatoes; simmer 30 minutes. Add peas, then flour blended with cold water. Cover and heat to boiling. Remove from heat. Top with dumplings; steam 12-15 minutes without removing lid. To make dumplings:

1 1/2 c. whole wheat flour
2 tsp. baking powder
1/2 tsp. salt
1 tsp. dried onions

1/2 c. raisins
1 egg
1/2 c. milk
2 Tbsp. safflower oil

Combine dry ingredients, add egg, milk and oil all at once. Drop by tablespoonfuls.

Preparation time: 3 hours   Yield: 6 - 8 servings

MEXICAN MEAT LOAVES

2 lb. lean ground beef
1 c. uncooked oats
2 eggs
1 (8 oz.) can tomato sauce
3 Tbsp. dried onions
2 tsp. chili powder

1 tsp. garlic salt
1 (4 oz.) can green chilies,
   drained and chopped
1 (8 oz.) can tomato sauce
1 c. shredded sharp cheese

Make a mixture of beef, oats, eggs, 1 can tomato sauce, onion, chili powder and garlic salt. Work with hands and mix well; shape into 10 small meat loaves. Place in a baking dish and bake for 20-25 minutes at 375 degrees. Meanwhile, combine chilies, 1 can tomato sauce and a dash of salt; heat to pour over meat loaves as they're done. Sprinkle with cheese; serve.

Preparation time: 45 minutes   Yield: 10 meat loaves

SWEET AND SOUR PORK

3 Tbsp. butter
3 lb. diced lean pork (use roast)
2 medium onions
1 c. celery
1/2 c. chopped green pepper
2/3 c. honey

1 (13 1/2 oz.) can pineapple chunks
  in own juice
3 Tbsp. oat flour (or other
  whole grain flour)
1/2 c. apple cider vinegar
1/2 c. water

Melt butter in a large skillet. Brown meat, add onion, celery and pepper. Cook about 30 minutes, covered, over medium heat, stirring often. Place honey, juice from pineapple, vinegar, water and flour in blender. Whirl until smooth. Add pineapple chunks and blended mixture to pork; continue to cook until sauce thickens.

Preparation time: 45 minutes   Yield: 4 - 6 servings

STUFFED ACORN SQUASH

2 acorn squash
1 lb. cooked, ground sausage
1 c. chopped, unpeeled apples
1 c. broken corn bread* crumbs
2 eggs
1/2 c. water
1/4 c. currants

2 Tbsp. chopped onion
2 Tbsp. chopped green pepper
2 Tbsp. chopped celery
1 Tbsp. parsley
1 tsp. sage
Salt and pepper to taste

Halve squash crosswise and remove seeds. Slice across the bottom of each piece just enough that squash will set squarely in baking dish. Brown sausage and drain; combine all other ingredients and season to taste with salt and pepper. Stuff squash and bake leftover stuffing in a casserole dish, pouring 1/2 cup additional water over the top. Bake, covered, for 1 hour at 350 degrees. Or, cover with plastic wrap and microwave on high for 12-15 minutes, until squash is tender.

Preparation time: 1 1/2 hours   Yield: 4 servings

DESSERTS

TENDER POUND CAKE

1 c. butter, room temperature
1 2/3 c. fructose
6 eggs, room temperature
2 1/2 c. unbleached flour

2 tsp. vanilla
1 c. heavy cream, whipped
    and unsweetened

Cream butter on high speed of mixer until very fluffy; add fructose and beat 2 minutes. Add eggs, beating 2 minutes after each one. Add vanilla and flour, stirring on low to mix. Fold in whipped cream and pour into greased and floured 9 X 5 inch pan. Bake for 1 hour or until done at 325 degrees.

Preparation time: 1 1/2 hours   Yield: 8 - 10 servings

ORANGE RUM CAKE

1 c. butter
3/4 c. fructose
3 eggs
3 tsp. orange extract
1 tsp. lemon extract

2 1/3 c. unbleached flour
2 tsp. baking powder
1 tsp. soda
1/2 tsp. salt
1 c. buttermilk

Cream butter and fructose; add eggs and beat thoroughly. Add flavorings. Add dry ingredients alternately with buttermilk, beating only until blended. Turn into tube pan which has been thoroughly greased and floured. Bake at 350 degrees for 45-55 minutes. Cool for a few minutes, then invert and cover with glaze.

Glaze:

1/2 c. fructose
1/4 c. orange juice

2 Tbsp. lemon juice
2 tsp. rum extract

Combine and heat until fructose is dissolved; spoon over hot cake.

Preparation time: 1 hour 15 minutes   Yield: 14 - 16 servings

APPLESAUCE CAKE

1 c. butter, no substitute
1 1/2 c. fructose
3 eggs
2 1/2 c. chunky applesauce*
1 Tbsp. soda
3 2/3 c. unbleached flour
1 Tbsp. salt

1 Tbsp. cinnamon
1 Tbsp. nutmeg
1 c. nuts
1 c. raisins
2 Tbsp. cocoa
1/3 c. apple juice concentrate

Cream butter and fructose; add eggs and beat until light. Mix soda with applesauce and add alternately with flour, salt, cinnamon and nutmeg. Add cocoa and mix well; stir in nuts and raisins, then turn into well greased and floured tube pan. Bake at 350 degrees for 1 - 1 1/2 hours. Cool 5 minutes, invert on wire rack, then on serving plate, and spray with apple juice concentrate.

Preparation time: 2 hours   Yield: 14 - 16 servings
    Hint: I keep a plant mister in the kitchen for uses such as spraying on the apple juice concentrate glaze.

SOUR CREAM POUND CAKE

2 sticks butter, no substitute
1 2/3 c. fructose
6 eggs
2 tsp. vanilla
1 tsp. orange extract

1/4 c. cream
2 3/4 c. unbleached flour
1/2 tsp. salt
1/4 tsp. soda
1 c. sour cream

Cream butter and sugar until very light. Add eggs, one at a time, beating 5 minutes after each one. Add flavorings and cream, then add dry ingredients alternately with sour cream. Turn into well greased and floured tube pan and bake at 325 degrees until done; about 1 hour.

Preparation time: 1 1/2 hours   Yield: 14 - 16 servings

BANANA-PECAN CAKE

1/4 c. softened butter or margarine
1 1/4 c. honey
2 eggs
1 tsp. vanilla
2 c. unbleached flour
1 tsp. baking powder

1 tsp. baking soda
3/4 tsp. salt
1 c. plain yogurt or sour cream
1 c. mashed, ripe banana
 (about 2)
1/2 c. chopped pecans

Beat butter until fluffy; drizzle in honey very slowly. Continue beating; add eggs. Stir dry ingredients together, then add, beating only until moistened. Add vanilla, sour cream, banana and pecans, and stir together on low speed. Turn to high speed and mix for 1 minute; pour into 13 X 9 inch greased pan. Bake at 325 degrees for 40-45 minutes or until done. Serve with sweetened whipped cream.

Preparation time: 1 hour   Yield: 12 servings

CHOCOLATE-ZUCCHINI CAKE

2 1/4 c. whole wheat flour
1/2 c. wheat germ
1/2 c. cocoa
2 1/2 tsp. baking powder
1 1/2 tsp. baking soda
1 tsp. salt
1 tsp. cinnamon
1 1/2 sticks butter or margarine
1 c. honey

3/4 c. fructose
3 eggs
2 tsp. vanilla
2 tsp. lemon peel
2 c. grated, unpeeled zucchini
1/2 c. milk
1 c. chopped nuts
1 c. raisins

Stir together dry ingredients; set aside. Cream butter, add fructose and beat well. Add honey and eggs, beat until creamy. Stir in vanilla, lemon peel and zucchini; then add flour mixture alternately with milk. Stir in nuts and raisins, then turn into well-greased tube pan and bake at 375 degrees for 45-50 minutes.

Preparation time: 1 hour   Yield: 14 - 16 servings

APPLE SNACK CAKE

1 c. whole wheat flour
2 Tbsp. unprocessed bran
1 tsp. soda
1/2 tsp. salt
1/2 tsp. cinnamon
1/4 tsp. nutmeg

2 c. shredded tart apples
1 c. honey
1/4 c. safflower oil
1/2 c. chopped nuts
1 well beaten egg
1/2 tsp. vanilla

Combine dry ingredients, stir in honey, oil and eggs. Add vanilla, then apples and nuts. Mix thoroughly and pour into 9 inch square, greased cake pan. Bake at 350 degrees for 35-40 minutes or until done.

Preparation time: 50 minutes   Yield: 9 servings

PINEAPPLE UPSIDE-DOWN CAKE

8 slices canned pineapple
  (natural juice pack)
8 walnut or pecan halves
4 Tbsp. melted butter
2/3 c. honey
1/2 c. butter or margarine
1 c. fructose

2 eggs
1 3/4 c. unbleached flour
2 Tbsp. wheat germ
1 Tbsp. baking powder
3/4 tsp. salt
2/3 c. milk

Arrange pineapple slices to fit a greased (6 1/2 X 10 inch) baking pan. Place a walnut in the center of each pineapple slice. Stir honey and melted butter together, then pour over pineapple slices. Cream 1/2 cup butter with fructose; add eggs. Add dry ingredients alternately with milk — do not overmix. Pour over pineapple and bake 40-45 minutes at 350 degrees. Turn out immediately onto serving dish

Preparation time: 1 hour   Yield: 8 servings

ALL-PURPOSE QUICK CAKE

1/2 c. butter
1 1/4 c. fructose
2 eggs
2 3/4 c. unbleached flour

2 1/2 tsp. baking powder
1 tsp. salt
1 1/4 c. milk
1 1/2 tsp. vanilla

Cream butter and fructose; add eggs and beat well. Add other ingredients all at once; stir until blended, then turn into greased and floured (6 1/2 X 10 inch) pan. Bake at 350 degrees for 30-40 minutes. Let stand in pan 5 minutes; invert and cool; frost.

Preparation time: 45 minutes   Yield: 8 servings
  Hint: Makes extra good cup cakes!

PUMPKIN BUNDT CAKE

1 c. safflower oil	1/2 tsp. soda
3 eggs	1 tsp. cinnamon
2 c. canned pumpkin	1 tsp. allspice
2 c. fructose	1/2 tsp. ginger
1/4 c. honey	1/2 tsp. cloves
2 3/4 c. unbleached flour	1 c. raisins
2 tsp. baking powder	1 c. nuts, chopped

Beat oil, eggs, pumpkin, fructose and honey until well mixed. Add dry ingredients and beat on medium speed for 1 minute. Stir in raisins and nuts; turn into greased and floured Bundt pan. Bake 1 hour at 350 degrees; cool 15 minutes and invert.

Preparation time: 1 1/4 hours   Yield: 1 tube cake
  Hint: Be sure cake has cooled completely before you invert.

OATMEAL CAKE

1 1/4 c. boiling water	1 tsp. vanilla
1 c. oats	2/3 c. whole wheat flour
1/2 c. butter or margarine	1/2 c. unbleached flour
1 c. fructose	1 tsp. cinnamon
1/2 c. honey	1 tsp. soda
2 eggs	

Combine oats and water. Let stand for 15 minutes. Meanwhile, cream butter, fructose and honey until light and fluffy. Add eggs and vanilla, then dry ingredients and oatmeal, stirring to mix well. Bake in a well greased (9 inch) square pan for about 50 minutes at 350 degrees. Spread topping mixture over cake:

2 Tbsp. butter or margarine	1/2 c. unsweetened coconut
1/2 c. honey	1/4 c. milk

Mix ingredients well, spread over cake and return to oven under broiler until toasted.

Preparation time: 1 hour   Yield: 9 servings

PRUNE CAKE

1 c. fructose
2 eggs
3/4 c. safflower oil
3/4 tsp. salt
3/4 tsp. soda
3/4 tsp. cinnamon
1/2 tsp. allspice

1/2 tsp. nutmeg
3/4 c. buttermilk
1 1/2 c. unbleached flour
1/2 c. chopped walnuts
1 c. cooked strained prunes
  (Jr. baby food size)

Beat eggs until light, add fructose and beat; add oil and stir. Add soda to buttermilk and mix alternately with combined dry ingredients. Add prunes and mix well; stir in nuts. Bake in a greased (9 inch) square pan for 45-55 minutes at 350 degrees or until done.

Glaze:

3/4 c. fructose
1/2 c. buttermilk

1/4 c. butter
1/4 tsp. soda

Simmer until dissolved (when bubbles are separated, mixture will be clear), and pour over cake as soon as it comes out of the oven.
(Making vertical knife slashes the width of your knife will ensure that the glaze soaks in well.)

Preparation time: 1 hour 15 minutes   Yield: 9 servings

MOIST APPLE CAKE

2 eggs
1 1/2 c. fructose
1 1/2 c. safflower oil
1 Tbsp. lemon juice
1 tsp. salt
2 tsp. vanilla

2 1/4 c. unbleached flour
1/2 c. whole wheat flour
1 1/4 tsp. soda
2 c. shredded tart apples
1 c. chopped dates
1 1/4 c. chopped nuts

Beat eggs well; add fructose and mix. Add oil, vanilla and salt. Combine flours with soda; stir into egg mixture. Stir in apples, dates and nuts. Turn into a greased and floured tube pan and bake at 325 degrees for 1 hour.
Preparation time: 1 1/2 hours   Yield: 1 tube-type cake
                                          (16 servings)
Hint: Glaze cake while hot with apple juice concentrate for an extra moist treat.

CARROT CAKE

1 1/2 c. safflower oil
1 c. honey
1/4 c. fructose
4 eggs
1 1/4 c. whole wheat flour
1/4 c. wheat germ

3/4 tsp. salt
1 1/2 tsp. soda
1 1/2 tsp. cinnamon
1 tsp. allspice
2 1/4 c. shredded carrots
1/2 c. chopped walnuts

Mix oil, honey, fructose and eggs until well blended. Add dry ingredients; blend thoroughly. Stir in carrots and nuts, then turn into well-greased and floured (6 1/2 X 10 inch) pan. Bake at 350 degrees for about 40-45 minutes or until done. Cool for a few minutes, then invert on rack for at least 30 minutes. Frost with cream cheese icing* if desired.

Preparation time: 1 hour   Yield: 8 servings

CREAM CHEESE ICING

10 oz. cream cheese,
   room temperature
1 Tbsp. milk

3 Tbsp. fructose
1 tsp. vanilla
1/8 - 1/4 c. honey

Whip cream cheese on high speed of mixer until very fluffy; add milk, fructose and vanilla; beat until very smooth. Add honey in a steady steam while mixer is running, adding until frosting reaches desired consistency.

Preparation time: 5 minutes   Yield: 1 1/2 cup frosting; will
                                           frost top and sides of a
                                           6 1/2 X 10 inch cake

Hint: Don't be alarmed if a yellow beaded substance appears on the frosting after a day or two — it's just the honey showing its color!

FUDGE CAKE

1/2 c. cocoa
1 c. boiling water
1 c. butter or margarine
1 1/2 c. fructose
3 eggs, room temperature

2 1/2 c. flour
Pinch salt
1 c. buttermilk
2 tsp. soda
1 tsp. vanilla

Dissolve cocoa in the water; cool. Separate the eggs, beating the yolks until thick and the whites until soft peaks form. Cream butter and fructose; add egg yolks. Stir in cocoa mixture, then add flour and salt alternately with soda and buttermilk. Add vanilla, then fold in egg whites. Bake in 2 (9 inch) round, greased and floured cake pans for 35-45 minutes at 350 degrees. Cook, then invert for 30 minutes before frosting with Fudge Icing.*

Preparation time: 1 hour   Yield: 1 (2 layer) cake

FUDGE ICING

1 stick butter (no substitute)
1 1/4 c. fructose
1/2 c. cocoa

1/2 c. milk
1 tsp. vanilla
1/4 tsp. lemon juice

Place butter, fructose, cocoa, and milk in a saucepan. Turn to med-high heat and bring to a boil, stirring occasionally. Boil one minute, then remove. Set pan in ice water and beat on high speed of hand mixer for 3-5 minutes. (Frosting will thicken and turn lighter in color.) Add vanilla and lemon juice and mix well. Spread on Fudge Cake* or Brownies*, etc.

Preparation time: 10 minutes   Yield: frosting for 2 layer cake

CHOCOLATE CREAM CHEESE ICING

6 oz. cream cheese
4 Tbsp. milk
1 tsp. vanilla
1/2 c. fructose

2 squares melted, unsweetened
   chocolate
Dash salt

Whip cream cheese, milk, vanilla, and fructose until light and fluffy; add chocolate and dash of salt and beat on "high" for 3 minutes.

Preparation time: 10 minutes   Yield: Frosting for 13 X 9 inch
                                              cake

DARK CHOCOLATE BUTTER ICING

1/2 c. butter
3 Tbsp. cream
1 tsp. vanilla
Dash salt

1 c. fructose
3 squares melted, unsweetened
   chocolate
2 egg yolks

Cream butter, cream, vanilla, salt and fructose for 3 minutes on high speed of mixer. Add egg yolks and chocolate; beat well. If texture is grainy, beat over hot water for a minute or so, (or put in microwave on high for 1 minute). Then beat until very thick over ice water.

Preparation time: 10 minutes   Yield: Frosting for 13 X 9 inch
                                              cake

RICH WHITE ICING

3 Tbsp. unbleached flour
1 c. milk
3/4 c. fructose

1 tsp. vanilla
1/2 c. butter
1/2 c. Crisco

Put flour and milk in the blender; whirl until smooth; then cook over medium heat until thickened. Cool for 20 minutes. Cream butter and fructose until very fluffy. Add vanilla and cooled flour mixture; beat until creamy and smooth.

Preparation time: 35 minutes   Yield: Frosting for a 2 layer cake
Hint: Delicious over chocolate cake or carrot-spice type cakes.

FOOLPROOF PASTRY

2 c. unbleached flour
1 tsp. salt
2/3 c. + 2 Tbsp. melted margarine

1 Tbsp. cider vinegar
1/3 c. cold water

Mix dry ingredients; cut in melted margarine until mixture resembles size of crumbs. Mix vinegar and cold water, add to flour mixture, tossing and stirring as you add. Stir vigorously with a fork until mixture holds together well, then form into a ball. Roll out between waxed paper sheets as needed. Chill 5 to 10 minutes.

Preparation time: 15 minutes.   Yield: Enough crust for 1 (10 inch)
                                              2 crust pie or 3 (9 inch) 1
                                              crust pies

STRAWBERRY PIE

3 pt. fresh strawberries
2/3 c. fructose
3 Tbsp. minute tapioca

1 (9 inch) pie shell*, baked and cooled
1 c. heavy cream, whipped and sweetened

Wash and cap strawberries. Place 2 cups strawberries in blender and purée. Combine puréed strawberries with 2/3 cup fructose and tapioca in double boiler. Stir over boiling water until thickened; 5-7 minutes. Remove from heat and quick-chill in ice water. Add remaining strawberries, folding into thickened mixture until all strawberries are coated. Turn into pie shell and cover with whipped cream; chill. (*FRUCTOSE FOR SWEETNER IN WHIPPED CREAM

Preparation time: 30 minutes   Yield: 1 (9 inch) pie; 8 servings

PUMPKIN PIE

1 1/2 c. pumpkin
3/4 c. honey
Pinch soda
1/2 tsp. salt
1 tsp. cinnamon
1/2 tsp. ginger
1/4 tsp. nutmeg

1/2 tsp. cloves
1 tsp. vanilla
4 beaten eggs
1 1/2 c. evaporated milk
1/4 c. melted butter
1 (10 inch) pie shell*, unbaked

Mix pumpkin, honey and seasonings; beat well. Add eggs, milk and butter and beat until thoroughly mixed. Pour into unbaked pie shell and bake at 375 degrees for 1 hour, or until knife in center comes out clean.

Preparation time: 1 hour 15 minutes   Yield: 1 (10 inch) pie; 8 servings
     Note: The honey will produce a shiny appearance on the top of the pie, as opposed to the matte appearance of a pie made with refined sugar. Be careful not to overbake because it doesn't look done.

SWEET POTATO PIE

1 c. mashed sweet potatoes, cooked
2/3 c. honey
2 beaten eggs
1 Tbsp. flour
1/2 tsp. cloves

1/2 tsp. salt
1/2 tsp. cinnamon
1/4 tsp. nutmeg
1/4 tsp. ginger
1 c. light cream
3/4 c. chopped pecans
9 inch unbaked pie shell

Blend sweet potatoes, honey and eggs. Add seasonings and cream. Stir in pecans and turn into 9 inch unbaked pie shell. Bake 50-60 minutes at 400 degrees or until done.

Preparation time: 1 hour 30 minutes   Yield: 1 (9 inch) pie; 6-8 servings

SOUR CREAM RAISIN PIE

3 eggs
1 1/2 c. dairy sour cream
3/4 c. fructose
1 1/2 tsp. vanilla

3/8 tsp. salt
1/4 tsp. nutmeg
1 1/2 c. raisins
1 (9 inch) pie shell*

Beat eggs, sour cream, fructose and vanilla until well-mixed. Add other ingredients and pour into pie shell; sprinkle with additional nutmeg and bake at 375 degrees until set, 40-45 minutes.

Preparation time: 50 minutes   Yield: 1 (9 inch) pie; 6-8 servings

PEANUT BUTTER AND HONEY PIE

4 eggs
1 c. honey
1/3 c. fructose
1/2 c. natural-style peanut
  butter

1/2 tsp. vanilla
1 c. chopped salted peanuts
1 (9 inch) unbaked pie shell*
1/2 pt. heavy cream
2 Tbsp. fructose

Beat eggs with honey and fructose; add peanut butter and vanilla and beat until creamy. Stir in peanuts and turn into 9 inch unbaked pie shell. Bake at 350 degrees for 1 hour, until toothpick in center comes out clean. Cool completely and refrigerate. Just before serving, whip cream, sweetening with 2 tablespoons fructose. Cover pie with cream and serve. (Top of pie will be hard; peanuts rise to the top and form a crunchy coating for the chess-type filling.)

Preparation time: 1 hour 15 minutes   Yield: (9 inch) pie, 8 servings

CHOCOLATE PIE

2 Tbsp. unsweetened cocoa
2 Tbsp. cornstarch
1/2 c. fructose
1/8 tsp. salt
2 c. half & half
3 egg yolks

1 tsp. butter
1 tsp. vanilla
1 baked (9 inch) pie shell*
3 egg whites
3 Tbsp. fructose

Stir cocoa, cornstarch, fructose and salt until smooth; add milk and stir with wire whip until creamy. Cook and stir over medium heat until thickened; remove from heat. Stir a small amount of hot mixture into egg yolks, then return to pan. Cook, stirring constantly for 2 more minutes. Remove from heat and quick-chill pan in ice water; add butter and vanilla, stirring to melt, and cool. Pour into shell and top with meringue made by whipping 3 egg whites until stiff peaks appear, then adding fructose and whipping to mix. Seal edges to crust and bake at 350 degrees for 12-15 minutes; cool completely.

Preparation time: 45 minutes   Yield: 1 (9 inch) pie; 8 servings

SOUR CREAM LEMON PIE

3/4 c. fructose
3 Tbsp. cornstarch
Dash of salt
1 c. milk
3 egg yolks
4 Tbsp. butter or margarine

1 tsp. lemon peel
1/4 c. lemon juice
1 c. sour cream
1 baked (9 inch) pie shell*
3 egg whites
3 Tbsp. fructose

Combine sugar, cornstarch and salt; stir until smooth. Stir in milk and whip with wire whisk until very smooth. Cook and stir over medium heat until boiling and thickened. Remove from heat; blend small amount of hot mixture into egg yolks; stir back into saucepan. Cook 2 more minutes, stirring constantly. Add butter, lemon peel, lemon juice, then quick chill in ice water, stirring to melt butter and cool mixture. When cooled, stir in sour cream and turn into pie shell. Whip egg whites until stiff peaks appear; add 3 tablespoons fructose and whip to mix. Spread over pie, sealing edges, and bake at 350 degrees for 12-15 minutes. Chill

Preparation time: 45 minutes   Yield: 1 (9 inch) pie; 8 servings

COCONUT CREAM PIE

2 c. half & half (or
  evaporated milk)
1/3 c. fructose
1/4 c. cornstarch
1/2 tsp. salt
3 egg yolks

2 Tbsp. butter
2 tsp. vanilla
1 c. unsweetened coconut
1 (9 inch) baked pie shell*
Sweetened whipped cream

Scald 1 1/2 cups milk; place remaining 1/2 cup in blender jar with fructose, cornstarch and salt. Mix well and add scalded milk to blended mixture while motor is running. Pour into saucepan and cook until thickened, stirring constantly. Remove from heat; add egg yolks to thickened cream mixture, stirring quickly with wire whisk until distributed throughout. Return to medium heat and cook, stirring constantly, for 3 more minutes. Quick-chill in ice, adding butter and vanilla, then coconut to cooling mixture. When cool, pour into pie shell, top with whipped cream and chill for several hours.

Preparation time: 30 minutes   Yield: 1 (9 inch) pie; 8 servings

DIFFERENT PECAN PIE

3 egg whites, room temperature
1/2 tsp. baking powder
1 c. crunchy granola* crumbs
2/3 c. fructose

1 c. chopped pecans
1 tsp. vanilla
1/2 pt. whipping cream
3 Tbsp. fructose

Beat egg whites and baking powder until very stiff. Combine granola crumbs, fructose, chopped pecans, and vanilla. Fold in egg whites and spread in a buttered 9 inch pie pan. Bake at 350 degrees for 30 minutes. Cool well, then cover with whipped cream sweetened with 3 tablespoons fructose. Chill thoroughly (4-5 hours).

Preparation time: 1 hour   Yield: 1 (9 inch) pie; 8 servings

BLUEBERRY PIE

Pastry* for 2 crust (9 inch) pie
6 c. fresh or unthawed frozen
   blueberries
3/4 c. fructose
5 Tbsp. flour

1 tsp. lemon peel
1 tsp. cinnamon
2 Tbsp. butter
Dash salt
1 Tbsp. lemon juice

Combine fructose, flour, lemon peel and cinnamon, and sprinkle over blueberries. Dot with butter and sprinkle woth lemon juice, then adjust top crust with steam vents. Bake at 400 degrees for 35 minutes.

Preparation time: 50 minutes   Yield: 1 (9 inch) pie; 6-8 servings

LEMON CHESS PIE

6 Tbsp. butter
1 1/2 c. fructose
6 eggs

1 1/2 Tbsp. white corn meal
6 Tbsp. lemon juice
Unbaked pastry for 9 inch pie *

Cream butter and fructose. Add all 6 eggs and beat well. Stir in corn meal and lemon juice, then turn into 9 inch prepared pie crust. Bake at 325 degrees for 40-50 minutes, until there is a golden crust on top.

Preparation time: 1 hour   Yield: 1 (9 inch) pie; 8 servings

COCONUT-CHESS PIE

Unbaked 9 inch pie shell*
3 eggs
1 c. fructose
1 stick butter, melted

Pinch of salt
2 tsp. vanilla
1/3 c. (heaping) coconut
1 Tbsp. cider vinegar

Beat eggs well; add fructose and beat until light. Add other ingredients and pour into 8 inch prepared pie shell. Bake at 350 degrees for 40 minutes.

Preparation time: 45 minutes   Yield: 1 (8 inch) pie; 6 servings

CHOCOLATE ICEBOX PIE

2 c. crunchy granola*
3 Tbsp. butter, melted
1 Tbsp. fructose
3/4 c. butter
3/4 c. fructose

2 1/2 squares unsweetened
  chocolate
1 1/2 tsp. vanilla
3 eggs
1 c. sweetened whipped cream

Place granola in blender and process until mixture has the texture of crumbs throughout. Put granola crumbs in a 10 inch pie pan, add 1 tablespoon fructose and stir to mix. Add melted butter, stirring with fork until all crumbs have been moistened. Press in the bottom and sides to form crust; chill in freezer. Melt chocolate; set aside. Cream butter until light and fluffy; add fructose and whip for 2-3 minutes. Add chocolate, vanilla and eggs, beating on high speed for 5 minutes. Pour into buttered pie plate and chill. Just before serving, top with sweetened whipped cream.

Preparation time: 20 minutes   Yield: 1 (10 inch) pie; 8 servings

LEMON MERINGUE PIE

4 Tbsp. cornstarch
1/3 c. fructose
1/4 tsp. salt
1 1/2 c. water
3 egg yolks

1/3 c. fructose
2 Tbsp. butter
5 Tbsp. fresh squeezed lemon juice
1 1/2 tsp. fresh grated lemon rind
9 inch baked pie crust*

Combine cornstarch, 1/3 cup fructose and salt in a saucepan. Stir in water, beating with wire whisk constantly and cooking over medium heat until thickened. Add egg yolks and 1/3 cup fructose, stirring constantly; cook 1-2 more minutes. Remove from heat and stir in butter, lemon juice and lemon rind. Cool, then pour into 9 inch pie shell baked and cool. Cover, sealing edges with meringue made from 3 egg whites and 3 tablespoons fructose. Brown meringue and cool completely.

Preparation time: 40 minutes   Yield: 1 (9 inch) pie; 6-8 servings

EASY COCONUT PIE

1 (9 inch) unbaked pie shell*
1 stick butter, no substitute
1 c. fructose
3 eggs

1 c. unsweetened coconut
1 tsp. vanilla
1 Tbsp. apple cider vinegar

Cream butter and fructose; add eggs and beat well. Add remaining ingredients and pour into pie shell. Bake 45 minutes at 325 degrees.

Preparation time: 50 minutes   Yield: 1 (9 inch) pie; 6-8 servings

EGG CUSTARD PIE

4 eggs
1/3 c. fructose
Pinch of salt
1 tsp. vanilla

1 1/2 c. milk, room temperature
1/2 tsp. nutmeg
9 inch unbaked pie shell*
(optional)

Beat eggs well; add fructose and beat until light and fluffy. Add salt, vanilla and nutmeg. Turn into pie shell or custard cups. Bake at 425 degrees for 10 minutes, then at 325 degrees for 15 minutes. Cool completely.

Preparation time: 45 minutes   Yield: 1 (9 inch) pie; 6 servings

PERFECT APPLE PIE

8 c. peeled and thinly
   sliced tart apples
3/4 c. fructose
3 Tbsp. unbleached flour

1 tsp. cinnamon
Dash of nutmeg and salt
3 Tbsp. butter
Pastry for 2-crust pie*

Prepare apples; place in a large bowl and toss with fructose, flour, cinnamon, nutmeg and salt. Put in pastry shell and dot with butter. Adjust top crust, allowing slits for steam to escape; seal and flute. Bake at 400 degrees for about 45-50 minutes or until done. Allow to stand at least 1 hour before cutting.

Preparation time: 1 1/4 hours   Yield: 1 (9 inch) pie; 6 servings

APPLE-HONEY PIE
Reprinted from Oct. 27, 1978 Family Circle magazine
© 1978 Family Circle Inc. (all rights reserved)

Crust for 2 crust (9 inch) pie*
3/4 c. honey
1/2 c. sour cream
4 Tbsp. flour
1/4 tsp. salt

1/8 tsp. ground cardamon
2 tsp. lemon rind
6 c. thinly sliced tart apples
1/2 c. golden raisins

Prepare crust; slice apples. Toss other ingredients with apples until well-coated. Pour into crust, cover with top crust and adjust with slits for steam. Bake at 425 degrees for 45 minutes or until pastry is golden and juices bubble up. Let stand for at least one hour before serving.

Preparation time: 1 1/2 hours   Yield: 1 (9 inch) pie; 8 servings

CRANBERRY DESSERT PIE

1 c. fresh cranberries   1/2 c. honey
1/4 c. fructose   1/2 c. whole wheat flour
1/2 c. chopped nuts   6 Tbsp. melted butter
1 egg   Sweetened whipped cream

Grease a 9 inch pie pan; place cranberries, fructose and nuts in it. Make a batter from remaining ingredients and pour over cranberries. Bake 40-45 minutes at 325 degrees. Serve in wedges topped with sweetened whipped cream.

Preparation time: 55 minutes   Yield: 1 (9 inch) pie, 8 servings

PEACH COBBLER

4 c. sweetened peaches (use   1/2 tsp. baking powder
   1/2 c. fructose to sweeten)   1/4 tsp. salt
1 stick butter or margarine   1/2 c. fructose
7/8 c. unbleached flour

Melt butter in square baking dish; make a batter of flour, baking powder, salt and fructose and pour over butter. Add peaches with juice and bake for about 40 minutes at 375 degrees.

Preparation time: 50 minutes   Yield: 1 cobbler, 8 servings

CUTOUT "SUGAR" COOKIES

1/2 c. butter, no substitute   1 tsp. cream of tartar
3/4 c. fructose   1/2 tsp. soda
1 egg   1/4 tsp. salt
1 1/3 c. unbleached flour   1/2 tsp. vanilla

Cream butter and fructose until very light; add egg and beat well. Add dry ingredients, then vanilla; stir and mix until dough holds together — chill. Working with small amounts of dough, roll out and cut into desired shapes. Cookies will taste best if rolled out thin and as little flour as possible is used. Bake at 350 degrees for 8-10 minutes; cool on wire racks.

Preparation time: 10 minutes   Yield: 3 dozen
        (for dough)

LEMON CURRANT COOKIES

1 stick butter or maragrine
2/3 c. fructose
2 eggs
1 Tbsp. milk
1 1/4 c. unbleached flour

1/2 tsp. baking powder
1/2 tsp. salt
1/2 tsp. vanilla
1 Tbsp. grated lemon peel
1 c. currants

Cream butter and fructose; add eggs and milk. Add dry ingredients and mix until blended; stir in currants. Drop teaspoonfuls onto greased cookie sheets and bake at 375 degrees for 12 minutes. Cool on wire racks.

Preparation time: 30 minutes   Yield: 3 dozen

PEANUT BUTTER COOKIES

1 stick butter or margarine
1/2 c. fructose
1/4 c. honey
1/2 c. natural-style peanut
  butter

2 eggs
1/2 tsp. vanilla
1 c. whole wheat flour
1/2 tsp. soda
1/4 tsp. salt

Cream butter, fructose, honey, peanut butter, eggs and vanilla thoroughly. Add dry ingredients and stir to mix. Drop by teaspoonfuls onto greased cookie sheets, flattening cookies slightly with palm of hand. Bake at 325 degrees for 10-12 minutes; cool on wire racks.

Preparation time: 30 minutes   Yield: 3 dozen

CRISP PEANUT COOKIES

1/2 c. butter, no substitute
1/2 c. natural-style peanut butter
3/4 c. fructose
1/4 c. honey
3 eggs
1/2 tsp. vanilla

3/4 c. unbleached flour
1/2 c. whole wheat flour
1 tsp. soda
1/8 tsp. salt
1/2 c. coarsely chopped, roasted
  and salted peanuts

Cream butter, peanut butter, fructose, and honey, then add eggs and vanilla. Stir dry ingredients in (except peanuts); mix well. Stir in peanuts and drop by teaspoonfuls onto greased baking sheets. Bake 12-14 minutes at 350 degrees.

Preparation time: 30 minutes   Yield: 3 1/2 dozen cookies
    Hint: These are good fresh out of the oven, but even better if allowed to stand several hours, tightly covered.

CRUNCHY COOKIES

1 c. whole wheat flour
1/3 c. powdered milk
1/4 c. wheat germ
1/4 c. unprocessed bran
1 tsp. baking soda
1 tsp. baking powder
1/2 tsp. salt
1/2 tsp. cinnamon
1/2 tsp. allspice

1/4 tsp. nutmeg
1/4 tsp. cloves
1 c. butter
1 c. honey
2 eggs
2 c. oats
1/2 c. chopped pecans
1/2 c. chopped dates

Cream butter and honey; add eggs; whip until very creamy. Add all other ingredients except for oats, pecans and dates. Mix until blended, then stir remaining ingredients in by hand. Drop onto greased cookie sheets and bake at 350 degrees for 10-12 minutes. Cool completely on wire racks.

Preparation time: 50 minutes   Yield: 4 dozen

CHEWY COOKIES

3/4 c. butter or margarine
1 1/2 c. honey
2 eggs
1/4 c. water
1 tsp. vanilla
1 c. whole wheat flour

1 tsp. salt
1/2 tsp. soda
1/2 t. cinnamon
3 c. oats
1 1/2 c. dried prunes, chopped
1 c. nuts

Cream butter and honey; add eggs, water and vanilla, beating well. Add flour, salt, soda and cinnamon, mix until blended. Stir in oats, prunes and nuts; turn into greased 9 X 13 inch pan. Bake at 350 degrees for 15-20 minutes, until mixture starts to set. Remove from oven, stir vigorously, and cool for a couple of minutes. Roll into balls and cool on wire racks.

Preparation time: 45 minutes   Yield: 6 dozen balls

CHOCOLATE DATE BARS

2 1/2 squares unsweetened
   chocolate
2/3 c; water
1 1/3 c. honey
3 c. chopped dates
1/4 c. butter or margarine
1 tsp. vanilla

3/4 c. butter or margarine
3/4 c. fructose
1 1/3 c. unbleached flour
1 tsp. soda
1/2 tsp. salt
1 1/2 c. oatmeal
1 c. chopped nuts

Melt chocolate, water and honey in saucepan or microwave; add 3 cups dates and cook 5 minutes on medium heat. Stir in 1/4 cup butter and vanilla; cool. Cream 3/4 cup butter and fructose; add flour, salt, soda, oatmeal and nuts. Press half of crumbly mixture in a greased 9 X 13 inch pan; cover with date mixture and top with remaining crumbly mixture. Bake at 350 degrees for 30 minutes.

Preparation time: 1 hour   Yield: 30 bars.

DATE BALLS

3/4 c. honey
2 eggs
1/2 c. unbleached flour
1/2 tsp. baking powder

1/4 tsp. salt
1 c. chopped dates
1 c. chopped walnuts
Unsweetened coconut

Beat honey and eggs until smooth; add other ingredients. Spoon batter into greased square pan and bake for 20 minutes at 350 degrees. Remove from oven and stir immediately; cool 5-10 minutes. With buttered hands, roll cooked mixture into balls, then roll in coconut. Cool completely, then store in tightly covered container.

Preparation time: 1 hour   Yield: 3 dozen date balls

ALMOND BARS

3/4 c. butter or margarine
1/2 c. honey
1 1/4 c. unbleached flour
1/2 c. wheat germ
1/2 c. oats
3 Tbsp. fructose
1/2 tsp. soda

1/4 tsp. salt
2 oz. unsweetened chocolate
1/3 c. fructose
4 Tbsp. butter
1/4 c. heavy cream
1/2 c. slivered almonds

Melt butter and honey in a small saucepan (or microwave 1 minute). Stir together flour, wheat germ, oats, 3 tablespoons fructose, soda and salt. Pour butter-honey mixture over dry ingredients and stir to moisten. Pat into a 6 1/2 X 10 inch or 9 inch square, ungreased pan; bake 10 minutes at 350 degrees. Meanwhile, melt chocolate, fructose, butter and cream in double boiler, (or microwave 3 minutes). Drizzle over baked layer, top with almonds and bake 10 more minutes.

Preparation time: 30 minutes   Yield: 16 bars

APRICOT FILLED COOKIES

Cookie Dough:

1 c. unbleached flour
1/2 tsp. soda
1/4 tsp. salt

1 c. oatmeal
1/2 c. butter
2/3 c. honey

Filling:

1/2 c. nuts, chopped
1/2 c. boiling water

1/2 c. dried apricots
1/3 c. fructose

Measure apricots and water into blender, chop for a few seconds until apricots have been chopped well. Let stand 15 minutes. Add fructose and nuts and process for 5 seconds. Cream butter, add honey, and dry ingredients, mixing well. Spread half the cookie dough in a 9 inch square pan that has been greased and floured. Follow with the filling, then top with remaining dough. Bake at 350 degrees for 30-35 minutes, cool and cut into bars.

Preparation time: 1 hour   Yield: 25 bars

GRANOLA BARS
(an easy not-too-sweet lunchbox treat)

1 1/4 c. crunchy granola*
1/2 c. raisins or dried fruit
1/2 c. chopped nuts
1/3 c. melted butter
3 Tbsp. fructose

1/4 c. honey
1 beaten egg
1/2 tsp. vanilla
1/4 tsp. salt

Combine granola, raisins and chopped nuts, stir in other ingredients and pat into 9 inch square, greased baking pan. Bake at 350 degrees for 20 minutes; cool, and cut into squares. Store in refrigerator.

Preparation time: 30 minutes   Yield: 16 bars

RAISIN BARS

3/4 c. butter or margarine
1/3 c. fructose
1/2 tsp. salt
1 3/4 c. unbleached flour
3 eggs
1 tsp. vanilla
1 c. honey
4 Tbsp. unbleached flour

1 c. raisins
1 c. unsweetened coconut
2 beaten egg yolks
3 Tbsp. fructose
Dash salt
1 c. milk
1 tsp. vanilla

Cream butter, fructose and salt. Stir in flour and pat into the bottom of a 13 X 9 inch pan. Bake at 350 degrees for 20 minutes. Meanwhile combine eggs, vanilla, honey, flour, raisins and coconut. Pour over first layer and bake another 20 minutes, or until set. While that is cooking, prepare a vanilla sauce by combining egg yolks, fructose and salt. Scald the milk, then gradually blend it into the egg yolk mixture. Cook until slightly thickened, stirring constantly. Cool; stir in vanilla; pour over raisin bars as they come from the oven.

Preparation time: 1 hour   Yield: 35 bars

CRACKED WHEAT CEREAL

1 c. cracked wheat
3 c. water
1 c. dates or dried prunes
1 c. light cream
1/2 c. nut pieces

1/4 c. fructose
1 tsp. cinnamon
1/4 tsp. lemon juice
1/8 tsp. salt

Combine cracked wheat and water in a saucepan; bring to a boil. Reduce heat; cook uncovered until water is absorbed, about 25-30 minutes. Remove from heat, and stir in dates or prunes, cream, nuts, fructose, cinnamon, lemon juice and salt. Serve hot as a cereal or cold as a pudding. Serve with additional milk or cream as desired.

Preparation time: 35 minutes   Yield: 4 servings

RICE PUDDING

1/2 c. powdered milk
1/4 tsp. salt
2 1/2 c. milk
2 eggs
1/2 c. honey

1/2 tsp. vanilla
2 c. cooked brown rice
1/2 c. raisins
Nutmeg

Combine dry milk and salt. Add milk, eggs, honey and vanilla; stir in rice and raisins. Turn into buttered casserole dish and sprinkle with nutmeg. Bake at 350 degrees, stirring once or twice for about 45 minutes, or until milk is absorbed. Best when served warm.

Preparation time: 1 hour   Yield: 4 - 5 servings.

DATE PUDDING

1 lb. pitted dates, cut up
1 c. boiling water
1 tsp. soda
4 Tbsp. butter
1 c. honey
1 beaten egg

1 tsp. vanilla
1/2 c. whole wheat flour
1 c. unbleached flour
3/4 c. chopped walnuts
Pinch of salt

Pour water over dates and add other ingredients. Stir by hand or on low speed of mixer until moistened throughout. Turn into buttered 10 inch pie pan, bake at 350 degrees until done, 30-35 minutes. To serve, cut as for pie and top with sweetened whipped cream. Delicious taste — similar to fruit cake but better!

Preparation time: 45 minutes   Yield: 8 - 10 servings

CARROT PUDDING WITH LEMON SAUCE

2 sticks butter or margarine	1/2 tsp. nutmeg
1 c. honey	1 tsp. baking powder
2 eggs	1 c. whole wheat flour
2 tsp. lemon rind	1/2 tsp. salt
1 tsp. cinnamon	1/2 tsp. soda
1 tsp. vanilla	2 c. grated carrots
1 tsp. orange extract	

Cream butter and honey; add eggs. Add other ingredients to mix, adding carrots last. Turn into well greased 5 cup soufflé dish or 5-6 individual dishes. Set in a pan of water and bake for 1 hour, (individual dishes for 30-35 minutes), at 350 degrees. Serve cold with Lemon Sauce.

Lemon Sauce:

4 tsp. cornstarch	2 Tbsp. butter
1/3 c. fructose	1/2 tsp. lemon peel
1 c. water	2 Tbsp. lemon juice
2 beaten egg yolks	

Combine fructose and cornstarch, add 1 cup water and stir until smooth. Cook over medium heat until thick, add egg yolks, stirring with mixer as you add, and cook 2 more minutes. Then add lemon peel and lemon juice and cool.

Preparation time: 1 1/4 hours   Yield: 6 servings

LEMON PUDDING

2 egg whites	1 1/2 tsp. grated lemon rind
3/4 c. fructose	1/4 c. fresh lemon juice
1/4 c. unbleached flour	2 egg yolks
1/4 tsp. salt	1 c. milk

Beat egg whites until very stiff, folding in fructose. Combine all other ingredients, then fold in egg whites. Pour into 4-6 individual custard dishes and set in a pan of water. Bake 20-25 minutes at 350 degrees until set. Chill.

Preparation time: 30-35 minutes   Yield: 4 - 6 servings

POPPY SEED COFFEECAKE

3/4 c. butter or margarine
1 c. fructose
4 eggs, separated
1/4 c. poppy seed
1 1/2 tsp. vanilla

1 3/4 c. unbleached flour
1 tsp. soda
1/4 tsp. salt
1 c. plain yogurt

Cream butter and fructose until light and fluffy; add egg yolks, poppy seed and vanilla. Add dry ingredients alternately with yogurt, then fold in stiffly beaten egg whites. Turn into well greased 9 X 5 inch loaf pan or 9 inch square pan. Bake at 350 degrees for about 45 minutes, or until done.

Preparation time: 1 hour   Yield: 9 servings

APPLE DUMPLINGS

2 1/4 c. unbleached flour
1/2 tsp. salt
2/3 c. cold butter
6-8 Tbsp. cold water
6 tart apples

1/3 c. fructose
1/4 c. milk
1/2 c. chopped dates
Honey

Make a pastry with first four ingredients; shape into 6 smooth balls. Roll each to a 6 inch square. Peel and core apples, enclosing each with pastry. Combine milk and fructose, and spoon into apple center. Stuff with dates and drizzle honey over top. Bake at 450 degrees for 15 minutes, then at 350 degrees for 30 more minutes or until done, basting every 15 minutes.

Preparation time: 1 hour 15 minutes   Yield: 6 servings

APPLE BROWN BETTY

2 c. crunchy granola* crumbs
  (blended fine)
3 Tbsp. melted butter
5 - 6 large apples

1/2 c. fructose
1/2 tsp. lemon peel
1 Tbsp. lemon juice

Stir granola crumbs with melted butter, making sure all crumbs are moistened. Place 1/3 of crumbs in the bottom of a buttered square baking dish. Peel and slice apples; place half of apples on granola. Mix fructose and lemon peel. Sprinkle half of mixture on apples; follow with crumbs and so on, ending with crumbs. Mix lemon juice with 1/3 cup hot water and pour over all. Bake at 375 degrees for 30-35 minutes; serve with sweetened whipped cream.

Preparation time: 45 minutes   Yield: 6 - 8 servings

SHORTCAKE

2 c. unbleached flour
1/4 c. fructose
3 tsp. baking powder

1/2 tsp. salt
1/2 c. melted butter (no substitute)
1 c. milk

Combine dry ingredients; add butter and cut in with pastry blender until mixture is the texture of fine crumbs. Add milk; stir until dough forms a ball. Turn into greased 9 inch pie pan and bake at 375 degrees for 20-25 minutes. Split and butter well; cool. Fill and top with fresh sweetened strawberries and whipped cream.

Preparation time: 30 minutes   Yield: 8 servings

ICE CREAM
(easy, creamy and quick!)

4 eggs, room temperature
1 1/2 c. fructose
1/2 tsp. salt
1 tsp. vanilla
2 c. heavy cream

1/3 c. fructose
3 pt. half & half
4 c. sweetened fresh fruit
   (optional)

Beat eggs until light; add fructose and beat well. Blend in salt and vanilla. Whip cream until light and fluffy, folding in 1/3 fructose. Blend into egg mixture and pour into ice cream freezer container. Add half & half to fill line and freeze according to directions. Pack in ice for 1 hour or place container in freezer.

Preparation time: 45 minutes   Yield: 1 gallon
    Hint: If fruit is used, add fruit after ice cream has frozen; use 2 pints half & half instead of 3.

COOL CITRUS YOGURT DESSERT

3/4 c. fructose
1 envelope unflavored gelatin
1/4 c. water
3 egg yolks
5 Tbsp. lemon juice

3 Tbsp. lime juice
2 c. plain yogurt
1 c. heavy cream, whipped
3 Tbsp. fructose

Combine fructose, gelatin and water. Stir in egg yolks, lemon and lime juices. Pour into double boiler and cook until slightly thickened, making sure gelatin is dissolved, (about 10 minutes). Cool slightly, then stir in yogurt. Pour into 9 X 5 inch metal loaf pan and place in freezer, stirring every 30 minutes or so. Freeze 2 hours. Remove from freezer and beat until smooth. Fold in whipped cream. Serve right away as a pudding or freeze 3 more hours and serve as ice cream (beat with mixer to make ice cream smooth, if desired).

Preparation time: 2 1/2 to 5 1/2 hours   Yield: 6 (1 cup) servings

MACAROON DESSERT

8 oz. whole blanched almonds
   (1 1/2 c.)
8 oz. walnut halves (2 c.)
2 egg whites, room temperature

Dash salt
2/3 c. fructose
1/2 c. butter or margarine,
   melted

Bake almonds and walnuts in a 375 degree oven for 20 minutes, until lightly browned. Meanwhile, beat egg whites until very stiff, folding in salt and fructose. Add nuts to meringue, then stir in butter. Bake at 350 degrees for 15-20 minutes, until lightly browned.

Preparation time: 40 minutes   Yield: 4 - 6 servings

CHOCOLATE VELVET CUP CAKES

3 squares unsweetened chocolate
1 1/2 c. fructose
1 stick butter, no substitute
3 eggs, room temperature

1/2 c. chopped nuts
1 tsp. vanilla
1/2 c. crunchy granola*

Melt chocolate. Cream butter, add fructose and combine with chocolate. Separate eggs, beating yolks until thick and lemon-colored, and whites until stiff peaks form. Add egg yolks to chocolate mixture; add nuts and vanilla. Place granola in blender and whirl until a crumb-like texture has been achieved. Sprinkle 12-14 paper lined muffin cups with crumbs. Fold egg whites into chocolate mixture and spoon carefully into paper lined muffin tins. Chill overnight or at least 8 hours. Serve with sweetened whipped cream.
Preparation time: 30 minutes + 8 hours Yield: 12 - 14 servings

HOT BANANA SOUFFLÉ

6 eggs
1/2 c. heavy cream
1 Tbsp. lemon juice
1 tsp. vanilla
1 Tbsp. orange rind

3 Tbsp. fructose
2 large, ripe bananas
11 oz. cream cheese
Sweetened whipped cream
(optional)

Butter a 5 cup soufflé dish, or 5-6 individual soufflé dishes. Place eggs, cream, lemon juice, vanilla, orange rind and fructose in blender; whirl until smooth. Cut bananas and cream cheese into pieces, add to blended mixture one at a time until mixture is creamy, then turn to high speed for 5 seconds. Pour into prepared dish and bake at 375 degrees for 45 (soft center), or 50 (firm center) minutes. Serve immediately with whipped cream.

Preparation time: 55 minutes   Yield: 6 servings

CURRIED PEARS

6 - 8 fresh pears
3 Tbsp. butter
1/3 c. honey

1/3 c. blanched slivered almonds
1 1/2 tsp. curry powder
Light cream

Peel pears; core and quarter. Place core side down in 1 1/2 quart baking casserole. Melt butter; add honey and curry powder. Stir to mix and pour over fruit. Top with almonds. Bake, covered, in a 325 degree oven for 1 1/2 hours. Serve warm with cream.

Preparation time: 1 3/4 hours   Yield: 6 servings.

POTPOURRI

MAYONNAISE

1 egg
1 Tbsp. apple cider vinegar
1/2 tsp. dry mustard
1/4 tsp. paprika
1/2 tsp. salt

1/8 tsp. cayenne
1 Tbsp. honey
1 Tbsp. lemon juice
1 c. safflower oil

Place egg, vinegar, dry mustard, paprika, salt, cayenne and honey in blender; whirl until smooth. With blender on lowest speed, add half the oil slowly, then the lemon juice and remaining oil. Continue mixing, scraping sides of blender, until oil has been distributed throughout for a creamy texture.

Preparation time: 5 minutes   Yield: 2 cups

Hint: This recipe can successfully be doubled, but when making large amounts of mayonnaise, do not triple.

TANGY CATSUP

2 1/2 tsp. cloves
2 inches stick cinnamon
2 tsp. celery seed
2 c. cider vinegar
3 (12 oz.) cans tomato paste
1/3 c. minced, dried onion
1 Tbsp. onion juice
1/4 tsp. white pepper

1/2 tsp. cayenne
1 tsp. salt
1/2 tsp. each cinnamon and allspice
1 1/2 tsp. cloves
1/2 tsp. dry mustard
1 tsp. chili powder
1 1/2 c. honey

Combine cloves, cinnamon, celery seed and vinegar in 2 quart saucepan. Bring to a boil, remove from heat and let stand 10 minutes. Strain spices, saving vinegar. Add other ingredients to vinegar, stir with wire whisk, and simmer on low heat for 20-30 minutes. Store in covered containers and refrigerate or freeze.

Preparation time: 45 minutes   Yield: 3 pints

SWEET PICKLES

1 (1 qt.) jar kosher dill spears	1 tsp. celery seed
1 1/2 c. honey	10 whole cloves
3/4 c. apple cider vinegar	1/4 tsp. garlic powder
1/4 c. water	Pinch alum

Drain pickles well; set aside. Combine honey, vinegar, water, celery seed and cloves in a small saucepan. Bring to a boil; add cloves, garlic and alum; pour over pickles and reseal; chill. Let stand at least 24 hours or longer for best flavor; save juice and use up to 4 more times.

Preparation time: 10 minutes   Yield: 1 quart pickles

CRISP PICKLES

8 large cucumbers	3 Tbsp. mustard seed
7 c. apple cider vinegar	1 Tbsp. turmeric
7 c. honey	1 1/2 tsp. alum
1 Tbsp. cloves	3 onions
2 Tbsp. celery seed	3 green peppers

Wash and slice cucumbers; cover and soak overnight in brine of 6 cups water and 1 cup salt. Drain; boil 5 minutes in syrup made of water, vinegar, honey, cloves, celery seed, mustard seed, turmeric and alum. Pack in hot jars; let stand 2 weeks.

Preparation time: overnight + 2 weeks   Yield: 3 quarts
                    standing time

PEPPER RELISH

2 - 3 green peppers	2/3 c. honey
2 medium onions	1 Tbsp. salt
2/3 c. apple cider vinegar	

Chop onions and peppers; cover with boiling water for 5 minutes. Drain and boil for 5 minutes in syrup made of vinegar, honey and salt. Pack in a hot quart jar; seal. Let stand for 1-2 weeks for best flavor.

Preparation time: 15 minutes + 1-2   Yield: 1 quart
                    weeks standing time

CRUNCHY GRANOLA

3 c. oats
1 c. wheat germ
1 c. sesame seeds
1 c. unsweetened coconut
1 c. chopped nuts

1 c. raisins (optional) or
   dried fruit
3/4 c. honey
1/4 c. oil
1 tsp. vanilla

Mix oats, wheat germ, sesame seeds, unsweetened coconut and nuts in large roasting pan. Mix oil, honey and vanilla and drizzle over dry ingredients, mixing with a fork as you pour. Bake at 350 degrees stirring every 5 minutes, for 30 minutes or until toasted. Cool completely and add raisins or dried fruit as desired. Store in tightly covered containers.

Preparation time: 45 minutes   Yield: 3 quarts cereal

PEANUT BUTTER GRANOLA

1/3 c. butter or margarine
1/3 c. natural style peanut butter

1/3 c. honey
2 1/2 c. uncooked oats

Melt butter, peanut butter and honey together in a saucepan; remove from heat and stir in oats. Bake on a cookie sheet for about 15 minutes at 350 degrees, or until golden. Cool and store, tightly covered, in refrigerator. Serve as a cereal with milk, or grind to a fine crumb in the blender and use in crumb crusts or to coat frozen bananas.

Preparation time: 30 minutes   Yield: 4 cups

CHUNKY APPLESAUCE

2 qt. cored, peeled and
   quartered apples
1 c. honey
2 tsp. cinnamon

1/4 tsp. nutmeg
Dash of salt
1 tsp. lemon juice

Place apples in a large Dutch oven and pour 1/2 cup honey over. Cook on low heat for 5 minutes, stirring frequently until juices form. Cover and cook on medium until tender, about 15 minutes. Mash apples with fork, potato masher or hand beater until desired consistency is reached. Season with additional honey, cinnamon, nutmeg, salt and lemon juice. Chill.

Preparation time: 30 minutes   Yield: 1 quart

Hint: This recipe may be multiplied to a bushel or more; when making that much applesauce, I usually substitute 1/4 - 1/3 cup of fructose for the last half cup of honey. I freeze mine, but it can be canned, processing in water bath for 20 minutes.

BISCUIT MIX

8 c. unbleached flour
1 1/3 c. powdered milk
5 Tbsp. baking powder

1 Tbsp. salt
1 c. vegetable shortening

Mix dry ingredients together; cut in shortening. Store in tightly covered container at room temperature for up to 6 weeks.

Preparation time: 10 minutes   Yield: 3 quarts mix

For biscuits:

2 3/4 c. mix   3/4 c. water

Knead lightly, roll, cut and bake at 425 degrees for 10-12 minutes. Makes 8-10 (2 1/2 inch thick) biscuits.

WHOLE-WHEAT PANCAKE MIX

4 c. whole wheat flour
4 c. unbleached flour
1 1/2 c. powdered milk
3/4 c. fructose

1/2 c. wheat germ
1/4 c. baking powder
1 Tbsp. salt
1 1/2 c. vegetable shortening

Mix dry ingredients together and cut in shortening. Place in a covered container and store in refrigerator for up to 6 weeks.

Preparation time: 10 minutes   Yield: 3 1/2 quarts mix

For pancakes, mix:

2 1/4 c. mix   1 beaten egg in 1 1/4 c. water

Bake on buttered griddle; makes 15 (3 inch) pancakes.
Hint: Add 1 cup cooked sausage meat to batter for _yummy_ sausage pancakes.

CRUNCHY CASSEROLE TOPPING

2 c. uncooked oats
1/3 c. wheat germ
1/3 c. Parmesan cheese

1/2 tsp. garlic salt
1/2 c. melted butter or margarine

Combine dry ingredients, drizzle butter over and stir to coat. Bake at 350 degrees for 15 minutes; or until golden brown. Cool; chop to a fine crumb in blender; cover and store in refrigerator or freezer. Use in place of bread crumbs or sprinkle over leafy salads.

Preparation time: 30 minutes   Yield: 3 cups

CRUNCHY CINNAMON TOPPING

1 1/2 c. uncooked oats
1/4 c. honey
1/4 c. butter or margarine, melted

1/4 c. wheat germ or chopped nuts
1 tsp. cinnamon

Combine all ingredients and stir constantly over medium heat until golden. Cool; chop in blender. Store in refrigerator or freezer and use as a topping for fruit salad, puddings, etc.

Preparation time: 15 minutes   Yield: 2 cups

MICROWAVE HOT CHOCOLATE
(You won't miss the marshmallows in this creamy mixture!)

For each serving:
1 (heaping) tsp. cocoa
1 (heaping) tsp. fructose
1 dash salt

1 c. milk
1/8 tsp. vanilla, if desired

Place cocoa, fructose, salt, and milk in blender; mix until smooth, about 30 seconds. Fill a glass, ovenproof ceramic, or other suitable micro-wave mug or cup full and cook on high for 1 1/2 minutes. (Or, pour into saucepan and heat until warm, do not boil.) Stir in vanilla and serve.

Preparation time: 2 1/2 minutes   Yield: 1 serving

DAIRY EGGNOG

1/2 c. fructose
4 egg yolks
2 qt. milk
2 egg whites

3 Tbsp. fructose
3 tsp. vanilla
1 tsp. brandy flavoring

Beat egg yolks, adding fructose and mixing well. Stir into milk and cook over medium heat, stirring constantly, until mixture comes to a rolling boil, about 30 minutes. Cool for 30 minutes and beat in egg whites which have been beaten to soft peaks with 3 tablespoons fructose. Add flavorings and chill thoroughly. Serve topped with nutmeg.

Preparation time: 1 1/2 hours +
                  cooling time

Yield: 8 cups

BOILED CUSTARD

6 egg yolks
1/3 c. + 3 Tbsp. fructose

6 c. milk
1 1/2 tsp. vanilla

Beat egg yolks and 1/3 cup fructose until thick; add 2 cups milk and beat well. Add remaining milk and pour into double boiler. Add 3 tablespoons fructose; stir over boiling water until mixture coats a wooden spoon, about 30 minutes. Remove from heat; cool slightly, and add vanilla. Store in jar or covered pitcher and serve ice cold.

Preparation time: 40 minutes +
                  cooling time

Yield: 1 1/2 quarts custard

AVOCADO-ORANGE BREAKFAST SHAKE

1 c. plain yogurt
1 c. cold water
1/2 c. orange juice concentrate
1/4 c. powdered milk
1 Tbsp. lime juice
1 Tbsp. lemon juice

1 Tbsp. honey
1/2 tsp. cinnamon
1 ripe avocado, peeled and
   cut in chunks
1 c. ice cubes

Combine yogurt, water, concentrate, milk, lemon and lime juice and honey in blender jar; process until smooth. Add avocado while motor is running, mix until smooth. Add ice cubes all at once and process on high until a slushy texture is formed. Serve at once.

Preparation time: 5 minutes

Yield: 4 - 5 servings

BREAKFAST SHAKE

1 1/2 c. orange juice
1 banana (frozen ones are nice)
1/4 c. powdered milk

1 egg (optional)
1 Tbsp. honey
6-8 ice cubes

Mix all ingredients together and whirl in blender until creamy throughout. Serve immediately.

Preparation time: 5 minutes   Yield: 1 quart

Note: Any leftover shake can be frozen in plastic "popsicle" containers for cool snacking.

YOGURT NOG

1 (8 oz.) carton plain yogurt
1 c. water
1 (6 oz.) can orange-pineapple
   juice concentrate

1/4 c. honey
1 egg
1 1/2 tsp. vanilla
10 ice cubes

Place all ingredients in blender; cover and blend on low for 30 seconds, then on high speed until mixed well.

Preparation time: 5 minutes   Yield: 4 servings

MINT PUNCH

2 c. water
1/2 c. honey
1/4 c. mint leaves

3 c. red grape juice
3 c. orange juice
3/4 c. lime juice

Bring water, honey and mint leaves to a boil; strain off mint leaves; combine with juices and chill.

Preparation time: 15 minutes   Yield: 1/2 gallon

CITRUS COOLER

2 (46 oz.) cans unsweetened
   pineapple juice
4 (7 1/2 oz.) bottles natural
   lemon juice or, juice of 24
   lemons

1 (16 oz.) can orange juice
   concentrate
1 c. fructose
1 qt. water

Combine juices; set aside. Add fructose to water and heat just long enough to dissolve fructose; add to juices and serve over ice.

Preparation time: 10 minutes   Yield: 5 quarts juice

GRAPE PUNCH

2 c. boiling water
1 c. fructose
2 c. strong tea
1 1/2 c. orange juice

3/4 c. lemon juice
2 tsp. almond extract
2 tsp. vanilla extract
1 qt. unsweetened grape juice

Add fructose to boiling water; boil 2 minutes. Add other ingredients plus 4 cups cold water. Chill and serve.

Preparation time: 10 minutes   Yield: 1 gallon

SPICED GRAPE DRINK

1 qt. bottled unsweetened
   grape juice
2 sticks cinnamon

1/2 tsp. whole cloves
1/2 tsp. whole allspice
2 Tbsp. fructose

Place juice and spices in a saucepan; bring to a rolling boil. Remove from heat and let stand, covered, for 5 minutes. Strain, add fructose and serve.

Preparation time: 10 minutes   Yield: 4 servings

CRANBERRY-APPLE DRINK

1 lb. bag fresh cranberries
2 (12 oz.) cans apple juice
1 tsp. allspice (optional)

1 tsp. cloves (optional
1 stick cinnamon (optional)
1/4 c. fructose

Wash cranberries; combine with 6 cups of water in covered saucepan. Bring to boil, and boil until skins pop. Set aside until completely cool, or chill in ice water. Strain skins off, saving juice. Process berries on mix speed of blender and strain into juices. (Add spices to juice; bring to a boil. Cover and steep 5 minutes; strain.) Chill juice, then add apple juice concentrate, two juice cans of water, and fructose. Serve piping hot or ice cold.

Preparation time: 3 hours   Yield: 90 ounces

SPICED TEA

4 qt. cold water
2 tsp. whole cloves
2 sticks cinnamon
2 tsp. whole allspice

15 tea bags
3/4 c. fructose
1 1/4 c. orange juice
3/4 c. lemon juice

Bring water and spices to a rolling boil; boil 5 minutes. Remove from heat and add tea bags immediately; brew 4 minutes, then strain. Add fructose and juices and return to heat until piping hot.

Preparation time: 25 minutes   Yield: 24 servings.

SUMMER CARROT COOLER

3/4 c. carrot juice
1 1/2 c. unsweetened pineapple
   juice
1/4 c. orange juice concentrate
1 1/2 c. orange juice
2 Tbsp. fructose

1 Tbsp. lemon juice
1 tsp. cinnamon
1/2 tsp. vanilla
Dash salt
8-10 ice cubes or
   2 c. crushed ice

Pour carrot and pineapple juices into the blender jar. Measure out 1/4 cup orange juice concentrate, then reconstitute the remaining juice. Add the measured concentrate, 1 1/2 cups juice, fructose, lemon juice, cinnamon, vanilla, and salt to carrot juice mixture, then whirl in blender. Add ice cubes or crushed ice and mix until ice is broken up. Serve immediately.

Preparation time: 5 minutes   Yield: 5 cups

TOMATO JUICE COCKTAIL

1 qt. tomato juice
1/4 c. lemon juice
1/4 c. lime juice
1/4 c. honey

1/2 tsp. celery salt
1/2 tsp. oregano
1/2 tsp. basil
1/2 tsp. onion salt

Combine lemon and lime juice, honey, and seasonings. Heat, covered, to boiling point, then combine with tomato juice and chill thoroughly. Serve over ice.

Preparation time: 5 minutes   Yield: 5 cups

SAUSAGE WHEELS

2 3/4 c. biscuit mix*   1 lb. uncooked sausage
3/4 c. cold water

Make a biscuit dough of the mix and water. Roll out to a large rectangle, spread with sausage. Roll up tightly, pinching ends to seal. To bake, slice in 1/2 inch slices and place on ungreased cookie sheet. Bake at 375 degrees for 25-30 minutes; or until done.

Preparation time: 35 minutes   Yield: 24 wheels
     Hint: These freeze nicely; one recipe makes 2 (12 inch) rolls. One may be frozen for later use if fresh sausage has been used. Good for breakfast; packable and good in lunch boxes too.

SAUSAGE BALLS

12 oz. sharp cheese, shredded   3 c. biscuit mix*
1 lb. uncooked sausage

Mix together well, shape into balls and bake at 375 degrees for 15 - 20 minutes, until tops are browned.

Preparation time: 30 minutes   Yield: 60 sausage balls
     Hint: I like to make up several recipes of sausage balls with fresh sausage and freeze them in groups of 1 - 2 dozen. These freeze nicely and may be baked at 425 degrees for 15-20 minutes from the frozen state. Great for breakfast or lunch boxes!

TUNA SPREAD

1 (9 1/4 oz.) can tuna
3 oz. cream cheese
1/4 c. mayonnaise*
1/4 tsp. garlic powder
1/4 tsp. celery seed
1/4 tsp. onion salt

Salt and pepper to taste
4 Tbsp. pepper relish*
1 Tbsp. lemon juice
1/2 c. sunflower seeds, roasted
  and salted
Few drops Tabasco sauce

Wash oil from tuna using hot water; drain well. Mix tuna, cream cheese and mayonnaise on low speed of hand mixer. Add other ingredients and mix well. Chill and use as a sandwich spread or dip.

Preparation time: 15 minutes   Yield: 2 cups spread

SHRIMP SANDWICH SPREAD

1 (8 oz.) pkg. cream cheese
1 Tbsp. onion juice
1 Tbsp. tangy catsup*
1 Tbsp. lemon juice
1 Tbsp. milk

1 tsp. parsley
1/4 tsp. chili powder
1/4 tsp. white pepper
1/4 tsp. salt
1 (4 1/2 oz.) can cooked shrimp

Whip cream cheese in mixer until smooth. Add all ingredients except shrimp and whip until smooth. Add drained shrimp and mix for a few seconds to crush shrimp. (Do not mix until smooth; should be lumpy.) Chill and spread on dark bread or wheat crackers.

Preparation time: 10 minutes   Yield: 1 1/2 c. spread

HOT CRAB DIP

1 can crabmeat
8 oz. cream cheese
1/2 c. evaporated milk
1/3 c. mayonnaise*
1 Tbsp. chives

2 Tbsp. green onions, chopped fine
1 Tbsp. parsley
1 Tbsp. lemon juice
Salt and pepper to taste
Tabasco sauce to taste

Place cream cheese, milk and mayonnaise in top of double boiler. Beat over boiling water with wire whip or hand mixer until creamy and smooth. Add crabmeat and seasonings; continue to heat until mixture is warm throughout. Serve with fresh vegetables.

Preparation time: 15 minutes   Yield: 3 cups dip

CRAB-CHEESE DIP

8 oz. grated Cheddar cheese
8 oz. process Cheddar cheese
6 1/2 oz. can crabmeat, drained

4 Tbsp. butter
Several dashes of Tabasco sauce
Several dashes of salt

Melt all ingredients over boiling water; serve hot with vegetables as dippers or spoon over baked potatoes.

Preparation time: 20 minutes   Yield: 3 cups

Hint: For microwave, place cheese and butter in baking dish. Heat on high for 5 minutes, stirring after each minute. Add crabmeat and seasonings, heat on high for 1 minute.

AVOCADO DIP SUZETTE

4 small ripe avocados, peeled
  and cubed
1 (8 oz.) pkg. cream cheese,
  softened

2 Tbsp. grated onion
1 Tbsp. lemon juice
Salt to taste
Tabasco sauce to taste

Combine all ingredients in blender; mix until creamy; chill. Delicious served with fresh vegetables.

Preparation time: 5 minutes   Yield: 2 cups

SHRIMP-CHEESE DIP

2 c. creamed cottage cheese
1 (3 oz.) pkg. cream cheese, cubed
3 Tbsp. Dijon-style mustard
3 Tbsp. mayonnaise*
2 Tbsp. dried chives
1 Tbsp. grated onion

1 Tbsp. lemon juice
1 tsp. honey
1/8 tsp. salt
1/8 tsp. pepper
2 c. cooked, cleaned shrimp
  (or 2 c. other desired filling)

Combine cottage cheese and cream cheese in blender and mix until smooth. Add seasonings and mix until very creamy. Pour into bowl and stir in shrimp, or chill. Delicious as a dip or served over baked potatoes.

Preparation time: 10 minutes   Yield: 3 1/2 cups

FRENCH DRESSING

1 1/2 c. safflower oil	1 1/2 tsp. salt
3/4 c. apple cider vinegar	1 tsp. paprika
1/4 c. honey	1/2 tsp. dry mustard
1 Tbsp. minced onion	1/4 tsp. black pepper

Place all ingredients in a blender; cover and process on high speed for 1 minute; chill.

Preparation time: 5 minutes   Yield: 2 1/2 cups

CHEF STYLE FRENCH DRESSING

1/3 c. fructose	1 tsp. paprika
1/3 c. honey	1 tsp. celery seed
1/3 c. apple cider vinegar	1 tsp. minced onion
1 Tbsp. lemon juice	1/4 tsp. salt
1 tsp. dry mustard	1 c. safflower oil

Mix all ingredients except oil in the blender; process until smooth. Slowly add oil through the top in a steady stream while motor is running. Process until oil is distributed throughout, about 1 minute.   Cover and chill. Use on "unmolded" gelatin salad or on any other salad where a French-style dressing would be used.

Preparation time: 5 minutes   Yield: 2 cups

DRESSING FOR SLAW

1 c. apple cider vinegar	2 Tbsp. mustard seed
1 c. honey	2 Tbsp. celery seed
1 c. safflower oil	1/4 tsp. white pepper
2 Tbsp. salt	

Boil vigorously for one minute; chill. Keeps 2 weeks in refrigerator.

Preparation time: 10 minutes   Yield: 3 cups

CREAMY BLUE CHEESE DRESSING

4 oz. Blue cheese
1/2 c. mayonnaise*
1/3 c. safflower oil
1/3 c. heavy cream
1/4 c. apple cider vinegar

2 Tbsp. honey
1/4 tsp. black pepper
1/4 tsp. garlic chips
Several dashes Tabasco sauce

    Combine all ingredients in blender; mix and chill, covered, for several hours for flavors to blend.

Preparation time: 5 minutes   Yield: 2 cups

TANGY RUSSIAN DRESSING

1 (6 oz.) can tomato paste
3/4 c. apple cider vinegar
1/2 c. safflower oil
1/4 c. honey
1 tsp. garlic salt

1 tsp. white pepper
1/4 tsp. savory
1/4 tsp. garlic chips
2 dashes Tabasco sauce
1 medium onion, cut in chunks

    Combine all ingredients in blender jar, cover and process on high 3 minutes.

Preparation time: 5 minutes   Yield: 3 cups

EASY HOLLANDAISE SAUCE
Recipe compliments of Oster Company

4 egg yolks
1/2 tsp. salt
1/2 tsp. dry mustard

1 Tbsp. lemon juice
Dash of Tabasco sauce
1 stick melted butter

    Put egg yolks, salt, mustard, lemon juice, and Tabasco sauce in Osterizer blender. Process until smooth. While motor is running on slow speed, drizzle butter through opening on blender cover. Mix until completely emulsified; serve at once or keep warm over hot (not boiling) water.

Preparation time: 5 minutes   Yield: 3/4 cup

LEMON SAUCE FOR VEGETABLES

2 Tbsp. butter
2/3 c. light cream or
  evaporated milk

1/4 tsp. salt
1 egg yolk
1 Tbsp. lemon juice

Combine the butter, cream and salt in a small saucepan. Stirring constantly, heat until butter melts. Beat egg yolk with fork, and spoon a small amount of the hot mixture into the egg, stirring quickly. Then return the mixture to the saucepan. Cook and stir until thickened; remove from heat and add lemon juice. Good over broccoli, asparagus and Brussels sprouts.

Preparation time: 10 minutes   Yield: 2/3 cup sauce

CRANBERRY SAUCE

1 (16 oz.) bag cranberries
1 c. water

1 1/4 c. fructose
(or 2 c. honey)

Wash cranberries and drain. Combine water and fructose with cranberries and bring to a boil. Continue boiling until the skins pop, about 5 minutes. Chill.

Preparation time: 15 minutes   Yield: 3 c. whole berry sauce

MUSHROOM SAUCE

4 Tbsp. butter or margarine
1/4 c. diced onion
1 c. fresh sliced mushrooms
2 Tbsp. whole wheat flour

1 c. light cream
1/4 tsp. salt
1/8 tsp. pepper

Sauté onions and mushrooms in butter until mushrooms are lightly browned. Combine flour, cream, salt and pepper in blender jar and mix until smooth. Pour into mushroom mixture and cook, stirring constantly, until thickened. Use in any recipe calling for condensed mushroom soup, or spoon over omelets or meats.

Preparation time: 10 minutes   Yield: 1 1/2 cups

LEMON-HONEY DESSERT SAUCE
(Must be served hot; ingredients will separate.)

1/2 c. butter or margarine
1/2 c. honey
1/2 c. half & half

3 Tbsp. lemon juice
1 1/2 tsp. lemon peel
1/2 tsp. vanilla

Combine butter, honey and cream; heat to boiling. Add remaining ingredients and serve hot, as a glaze over warm cake, or a sauce.

Preparation time: 5 minutes   Yield: 2 cups

ORANGE DESSERT SAUCE

1 c. orange juice
1/3 c. honey
1 Tbsp. cornstarch

Pinch of salt
1 Tbsp. butter

Combine orange juice, honey, cornstarch and salt; mix in blender jar or whip with wire whisk until smooth. Bring to a boil over medium high heat; remove from heat and stir in butter. Serve hot or cold over pound cake.

Preparation time: 10 minutes   Yield: 1 1/2 cups

HOT FRUIT COMPOTE

3 c. assorted dried fruit (choose
    from apricots, peaches,
    nectarines, apples, prunes)

1 c. golden raisins
Honey to taste

Wash fruits, and soak overnight in water to cover. Simmer until the fruits are plump and the water has cooked down to a medium consistency. Add honey to taste, probably 2-4 tablespoons will be plenty. Serve warm with cream.

Preparation time: 8-12 hours +   Yield: 6 servings
                 20 minutes

CHOCOLATE FONDUE

6 (1 oz.) squares unsweetened
   chocolate
1 1/2 c. fructose
1/2 c. butter or margarine

1/8 tsp. salt
2/3 c. light cream
1 Tbsp. rum flavoring

    Combine all ingredients and heat over boiling water until melted, then beat until creamy (or place in microwave for 5 minutes on high, then beat until creamy). Pour into chafing dish and serve with chunks of banana or apple or bite-sized pieces or pound cake.

Preparation time: 15 minutes   Yield: 4 - 5 servings

KID'S CORNER

OLD FASHIONED LEMONADE

2 qt. water
1 1/2 c. lemon juice

1 1/2 c. honey
1 c. water

1. Mix 2 quarts water and lemon juice; set aside.

2. Pour honey and 1 cup water into a saucepan and heat until it boils.

3. Add the honey mixture to the lemon juice and water; chill in the refrigerator.

4. To serve, stir, and pour lemonade over ice cubes. Decorate with slices of lemon.

Preparation time: 10 minutes   Yield: 3 quarts

PIMENTO CHEESE

3/4 c. canned evaporated milk
1/3 c. mayonnaise*
1/2 tsp. salt

1 dash Tabasco sauce
12 oz. Cheddar cheese, cut in cubes
1 small jar sliced pimentoes

1. Combine milk, mayonnaise, salt and Tabasco in the blender. Cover and mix on a low speed for about 1 minute. Turn off the blender.

2. Remove the center part of the blender lid, or remove the whole lid. Start the motor on a low speed and drop in the cheese cubes, one at a time. Be sure you wait a few seconds between cheese cubes so that the blender can mix up the cheese well. (At first the mixture might splatter, so cover the opening of the blender lid with your hand.)

3. Turn off the blender; stir the cheese. Cover, and turn on the blender motor. Continue doing this until all the cheese cubes have been blended and the mixture is creamy.

4. Pour into a dish, drain the pimentoes and stir them into the cheese.

5. Stuff cheese into celery or spread on your favorite crackers or bread; cover and chill to serve later.

Preparation time: 15 minutes   Yield: 2 cups

YUMMY BAKED EGGS

For each serving:
1 Tbsp. butter or margarine   **1 egg**
1 slice Swiss cheese   **Salt and pepper**

1. Set the oven on 350 degrees.

2. Place the butter in a casserole dish big enough for one serving, then put it in the oven until it melts.

3. Put the slice of cheese on the melted butter.

4. Break the egg onto a saucer, then slide it on top of the cheese. Sprinkle with a little salt and pepper.

5. Bake uncovered, for 12 minutes, or microwave 1 1/2 minutes on high.

Preparation time: 15 minutes   Yield: 1 serving

EASY PIZZA

1 1/4 c. unbleached flour   **1 tsp. salt**
3/4 c. oat flour   **2/3 c. milk**
1 tsp. baking powder   **1/4 c. oil**

1. Stir together the flours, baking powder and salt in a mixing bowl.

2. Pour the milk and oil into the flour mixture and stir until the dough holds together in a ball.

3. Squeeze the dough with both hands several times, then pat and spread into a 14 inch round pizza pan.

4. Bake at 425 degrees for 12-14 minutes.

Pizza Topping:

2 cans Chef-Boy-Ar-Dee Pizza   **2 c. grated Mozzarella cheese**
  Sauce with cheese   **1/2 c. Parmesan cheese**
3 c. cooked ground beef or sausage

1. Top crust with pizza sauce.

2. Spoon meat on, then cheese.

3. Sprinkle Parmesan on top, bake at 425 degrees for 10-15 minutes.

Preparation time: 45 minutes   Yield: 1 (14 inch) pizza

(This was the only pizza sauce without sugar; however it does contain modified food starch. But, I included it for ease of preparation. The adult or older child making this recipe can make a delicious pizza sauce by combining:)

1 (15 oz.) can tomato sauce   **1 tsp. salt**
1 Tbsp. Italian seasoning   **1 tsp. dried onion**
1 tsp. honey   **1/2 tsp. oregano**

DOUBLE CHEESE SANDWICH

2 thin slices favorite whole
  grain bread
1 slice American cheese

1 slice Swiss cheese
Mayonnaise*

1. Spread bread with a small amount of mayonnaise.

2. Place a slice each of American cheese and Swiss cheese on top of one side, put the "lid" on.

3. Put sandwich on a plate and heat in the microwave oven on high for 1 minute.

Preparation time: 3 minutes   Yield: 1 serving

BUTTER

1 c. whipping cream   **1/4 tsp. salt**

1. Set the cream out of the refrigerator and wait 30 minutes.

2. Whip the cream for 5 minutes with an electric hand mixer. Watch it get fluffy, then curdly.

3. Pour the curdled cream into a large strainer and stir it around a bit with a spoon. (The watery substance should stop dripping in a minute or two.)

4. Spoon the butter back into a clean small bowl, and add the salt. Stir it into the butter and be sure it is mixed well.

5. Spread the butter on your favorite whole grain cracker or bread — yum! If there is any left, cover it and put it in the refrigerator.

Preparation time: 10 minutes   Yield: 1/4 cup

EASY HONEY BUNS
(A favorite of our "Pooh-Bear")

1 pan of homemade rolls*,
  ready to bake
1/4 c. chopped peanuts

1/4 c. honey
2 Tbsp. butter or margarine

1. Have your mother bake the rolls as she had planned, but remove them 5 minutes before they are done.

2. Chop the peanuts in a nut chopper or blender.

3. Melt the honey and butter in a small saucepan or place it in a microwave oven on high for 1 minute.

4. Add the peanuts to the melted honey mixture and spread on the nearly-done rolls.

5. Return the rolls to the oven for 5 minutes—enjoy while hot with butter.

Preparation time: 30 minutes   Yield: 1 pan of buns

FROZEN BANANA POPS

6 firm bananas
1/4 c. honey
1/2 c. water

1/2 c. crunchy granola* crumbs or
    crunchy cinnamon topping*
6 wooden sticks or plastic skewers

1. Peel bananas. Stick a skewer into the end of each one and place in the freezer for 30 minutes.

2. Combine the water and honey. Roll the frozen bananas in it, then in the granola crumbs. Freeze in a plastic bag until firm.

Preparation time: 40 minutes   Yield: 6 banana pops

FROZEN YOGURT POPS

1/2 c. crunchy granola* or
    chopped nuts
4 c. flavored yogurt

6 (4 oz.) paper cups
6 "ice cream" sticks

1. Sprinkle a little granola in each cup.

2. Fill each cup halfway with yogurt.

3. Spoon the rest of the granola into each cup, and fill up with yogurt.

4. Smooth the top of each full cup with a knife, then place an ice cream stick in the yogurt. Push it about halfway to the bottom.

5. Freeze the pops for several hours, covering them with plastic wrap after the sticks are frozen securely in place.

6. To serve, peel the paper off the pops and enjoy.

Preparation time: 10 minutes   Yield: 6 pops

PEACHY YOGURT SUNDAE

3 c. plain yogurt
2 c. sliced peaches
1/3 c. fructose
1/2 tsp. vanilla extract

1/4 tsp. almond extract
1 c. fresh peach slices
1/2 c. crunchy cinnamon topping*
6 dessert glasses

1. Spoon the yogurt, 2 cups of peaches, fructose and flavorings into the blender jar. Cover and mix on a low speed until it is smooth.

2. Place two or three peach slices in the bottom of each dessert glass.

3. Fill each glass halfway with yogurt.

4. Put 2 peach slices on top of the yogurt, then fill up with yogurt.

5. Chill in refrigerator and top with crunchy cinnamon topping just before serving.

Preparation time: 20 minutes   Yield: 6 sundaes

POPCORN SNACK MIX
(Sticky, but good!)

2 qt. freshly popped corn	1 tsp. cinnamon
3 Tbsp. butter or margarine	1 c. raisins
1/4 c. honey	1 c. raw cashews
1 Tbsp. lemon peel	1 c. sunflower seeds

1. Melt butter with honey, lemon peel and cinnamon in a small saucepan.

2. Drizzle melted butter mixture over popcorn and stir until the popcorn is coated with butter.

3. Add the raisins, cashews and sunflower seeds; stir and serve.

Preparation time: 10 minutes   Yield: 6 - 8 servings

CURRIED SNACK MIX

1 (8 oz.) pkg. natural-style corn chips	1 stick of butter or margarine
1 c. whole or broken walnuts	1 1/2 tsp. garlic salt
1 c. whole or broken pecans	1 tsp. curry powder
2 qt. freshly popped corn	1/2 tsp. salt
	2 dashes of Tabasco sauce

1. Set the oven on 300 degrees.

2. Mix the corn chips, walnuts, pecans, and popcorn in a large bowl.

3. Melt the butter in a small saucepan, then add the garlic salt, curry powder, salt and Tabasco sauce.

4. Drizzle the butter mixture onto the popcorn and nuts; stir until the seasonings are mixed well.

5. Bake for 30 minutes, stirring every 10 minutes.

6. Cool and store in tightly covered jars.

Preparation time: 40 minutes   Yield: 5 quarts

FAVORITE SNACK MIX

1/2 c. roasted, salted pumpkin
   seeds
1/2 c. coarsely chopped walnuts
1/2 c. roasted, salted sunflower
   seeds

1/2 c. raisins
1/2 c. unsweetened coconut
1/2 c. chopped dates
1/2 c. chopped dried peaches

1. Measure all ingredients and toss with your hands in a large bowl.
2. Pour into jars or plastic containers.
3. Cover tightly and refrigerate.

Preparation time: 15 minutes   Yield: 4 cups

EMERGENCY SNACK

1/2 c. roasted peanuts   1/2 c. raisins

1. Measure peanuts and raisins and pour into a glass jar. Put on the lid.
2. Shake the jar until the peanuts and raisins are mixed well.
3. Remove the lid and share with friends.

Preparation time: 3 minutes   Yield: 3/4 cup

DATE SURPRISES

12 whole dates   12 whole natural almonds

1. Split each date down one side and remove the seed.
2. Stuff an almond into the hole where the seed was and pinch the edges of the date back together.
3. Serve at once to friends or store, covered in the refrigerator.

Preparation time: 15 minutes   Yield: 12 surprises

EASY CHRISTMAS CANDY
(Surprisingly delicious!)

1/2 c. honey
1 stick of butter or margarine

2 c. finely chopped nuts
1 tsp. vanilla extract

1. Melt the honey and butter together in a saucepan over medium heat.

2. Remove the saucepan from the heat and add the nuts and vanilla. Stir well.

3. When the mixture is cool enough to handle, shape into balls or sticks. (Be sure and butter your hands often so the candy won't stick.)

4. Place the candy on a tray and cover well with plastic wrap. Put it in the refrigerator and chill until it is very firm.

Preparation time: 30 minutes   Yield: 2 dozen

Hint: Try the same directions using 1/2 cup natural style peanut butter instead of the butter and 2 cups of chopped peanuts for the nuts. Keep the amounts of honey and vanilla the same.

PEACH CANDY

2 Tbsp. softened butter or
  margarine
1/2 c. honey
1 Tbsp. water
1/2 tsp. vanilla extract

1/4 tsp. almond extract
2/3 c. powdered milk
3 (10 oz.) pkg. dried peaches
2 c. unsweetened coconut

1. Ask your mother to run the peaches through the fine blade of the food grinder.

2. Put the butter, honey, water, vanilla, almond, powdered milk and peaches in a large bowl. Stir well.

3. Add the coconut and mix with your hands.

4. Shape into balls, rolling between the palms of your hands until they are smooth. It may be necessary to grease your hands with butter.

5. Chill well, covered, in the refrigerator.

Preparation time: 30 minutes   Yield: 2 - 2 1/2 dozen

PEANUT BUTTER BALLS

1/2 c. natural style peanut
   butter
1/2 c. powdered milk
1/2 c. honey

1 c. sunflower seeds
1/2 c. uncooked oats
1/2 c. unsweetened coconut

1. Place peanut butter, milk and honey in a saucepan and heat slightly. Do not boil, just heat to a point where the mixture is easy to stir.

2. Add sunflower seeds and oats; stir well.

3. Butter your hands and shape the mixture into balls.

4. Roll the balls in unsweetened coconut, then put them in the refrigerator. Cover the candy well.

Preparation time: 15 minutes   Yield: 2 1/2 - 3 dozen

DATE CANDY

1 (8 oz.) pkg. pitted dates
1 c. pecans

2 c. raisins

1. Ask your mother to run these ingredients through the fine blade of the food grinder. If she alternates the dates and raisins with the pecans, it will be an easier job.

2. Butter your hands and shape the mixture into balls, rolling several times between the palms of your hands until the balls are smooth.

3. Cover and chill the candy.

Preparation time: 20 minutes   Yield: 3 dozen

APRICOT FRUIT BALLS

1 box golden raisins
1 bag dried apricots

1 c. roasted peanuts

1. Ask your mother or an older person to chop these ingredients with the fine blade of the food chopper.

2. Mix well and roll into balls.

3. Store, covered, in the refrigerator.

Preparation time: 20 minutes   Yield: 3 dozen balls

PEANUTTY PUDDING

1 c. raw oats   1/4 c. honey
3/4 c. milk   1/4 tsp. salt
1/2 c. chopped peanuts   1 c. unsweetened whipped cream
1/3 c. 100% peanut butter

1. Combine the oats, milk, chopped peanuts, peanut butter, honey and salt in a large bowl.

2. Stir the mixture until everything is mixed up very well.

3. Put a lid on the bowl, or cover it with aluminum foil. Place it in the refrigerator, and wait 4 or 5 hours. (You may want to make this up the night before you want to eat it.)

4. Unwrap the pudding or remove the lid. You will notice that it is thicker; this is because of the oats.

5. Get out the whipped cream and add it gently to the pudding. Stir it carefully with a spatula, then chill again, or serve.

Preparation time: 10 minutes +   Yield: 6 servings
                  4 - 5 hours

CHOCOLATE-Y PUDDING

1 c. raw oats   1/4 c. honey
3/4 c. milk   1/4 tsp. salt
1/2 c. chopped nuts   1 c. unsweetened whipped cream
3 Tbsp. unsweetened cocoa

1. Stir the oats, milk, nuts, cocoa, honey and salt together in a large bowl.

2. Put a lid on the bowl or cover it with aluminum foil. Place it in the refrigerator and wait 4-5 hours or overnight.

3. Remove the pudding from the refrigerator and uncover it. Stir the whipped cream into the pudding carefully.

4. When the whipped cream and chocolate pudding have been mixed well, return to the refrigerator, or serve.

Preparation time: 10 minutes +   Yield: 6 servings
                  4 - 5 hours

MOIST APPLE "PIE"

2 eggs
1 c. fructose
1 c. unbleached flour
2 tsp. baking powder
1/2 tsp. salt

1 tsp. cinnamon
1/2 tsp. cloves
2 tsp. vanilla
3 c. chopped apples
3/4 c. chopped nuts

1. Set the oven on 350 degrees.

2. Break the eggs into a saucer, then slide them into a mixing bowl.

3. Beat the eggs with an electric mixer until they are well mixed, about 1 minute.

4. Add the fructose to the eggs and beat 2 minutes.

5. Add the flour, baking powder, salt, cinnamon and cloves. Beat very slowly until the ingredients start to mix up, then beat on a high speed for 1 minute.

6. Stir in the vanilla, apples and nuts with a large spoon.

7. Peel a little paper off a stick of butter or margarine and cover a 10 inch pie plate with butter.

8. Pour in the cake mixture and bake for 35-40 minutes, until a toothpick comes out clean when you stick it in the middle.

Preparation time: 1 hour   Yield: 8 servings

BROWNIES

2 sticks butter or margarine
3 squares unsweetened chocolate
6 eggs
1 1/2 c. fructose

1 c. unbleached flour
1/4 tsp. baking powder
1/2 c. chopped nuts
Spray vegetable coating

1. Set oven on 325 degrees.

2. Melt the butter and chocolate over boiling water in a double-boiler pot. (Or you can do it in the microwave on high for 4 minutes — be sure and stir it several times.)

3. While you are waiting for the chocolate to melt, break the eggs into a medium sized bowl. Make sure there are no shells with the eggs.

4. Take the chocolate and butter mixture away from the hot water. Add the fructose, flour and baking powder to the chocolate and beat for 1 minute with an electric hand mixer or spoon.

5. Add the eggs and beat for another minute.

6. Stir the nuts into the chocolate mixture.

7. Spray a 6 X 10 inch pan with a non-stick vegetable spray and pour the batter in.

8. Bake for 25 minutes, cool for a few minutes, then cut into squares and cover with foil, or serve.

Preparation time: 35 minutes   Yield: 12 brownies

LUNCHBOX CHOCOLATE CAKE

1 c. unbleached flour
1 c. whole wheat flour
1/4 c. unsweetened cocoa
1 tsp. baking powder
1/2 tsp. baking soda

1 c. mayonnaise*
1 c. honey
1 c. cold water
1 tsp. vanilla
Spray vegetable coating

1. Set the oven on 350 degrees.

2. Get a large bowl, and measure the unbleached and whole wheat flours, and the cocoa, baking powder and salt into it. Stir it around a bit until it is mixed up.

3. Pour the mayonnaise, honey, water and vanilla into the mixing bowl. Stir it with the spoon until it is mixed up, and then beat it for 1 minute with an electric mixer.

4. Spray a square cake pan with a vegetable spray, then pour in the cake batter. Smooth it over with a spatula, then bake for 30 minutes.

5. As soon as the cake comes out of the oven, cover the top with foil. After it cools, cut it into squares and pour yourself a glass of cold milk — invite a friend over if you wish.

Preparation time: 40 minutes   Yield: 9 servings

BREAKFAST
MENUS

23. Easy Pizza*
    tomato slices
    hot beef broth

24. Eggs and Mushrooms* (Q)
    Perfect Biscuits*
    Cold Fruit Soup*

25. celery stuffed with Pimento Cheese* or peanut butter (Q)
    shredded wheat crackers
    Frozen Banana Pops* (Q)

26. Baked Eggs with Chicken Livers*
    Buttermilk Whole Wheat Biscuits*
    fresh blackberries

27. assorted cheese slices
    Crunchy Granola* with milk (Q)
    fresh nectarine slices

28. Cheddar Cheese Soufflé*
    Easy Honey Buns*
    Orange-Grapefruit Salad with Avocado Dressing*

29. Avocado-Orange Breakfast Shake* (Q)
    Breakfast Crunchies*

30. Apricot Bread* toasted and spread with pot cheese (Q)
    Peachy Yogurt Sundae*

31. Hot Potato Soufflé*
    Blueberry Brancakes* with honey
    Grapefruit Compote*

32. Sausage Balls*
    Summer Carrot Cooler* (Q)
    fresh pineapple spears

33. sausage and scrambled eggs (Q)
    Apple Pancakes*
    Yogurt Pops* (Q)

34. farmer cheese broiled on Cracked Wheat Bread* (Q)
    Winter Citrus Salad*
    grapefruit juice

35. assorted slices of Mozzarella, Colby and American cheese
    Bran Muffins* (Q)
    fresh plums, apricots and cherries

36. Oatmeal with raisins and cream (Q)
    poached eggs on Whole Wheat Rusks*

37. Cream of wheat with chopped dried prunes or dates
    soft-boiled eggs and whole grain toast

38. French toast made from Bran Bread*
    cheese omelet
    tangerine sections

MAIN DISHES, SOUP

MAIN DISHES, TURKEY

MIXES

PIES

PUDDINGS

Please send me the following items from the *Feasting . . . Naturally* collection:

_____ Copies of *Feasting . . . Naturally* at $7.95 . . . . . _____

_____ Copies of *Feasting Naturally . . . From Your Own Recipes* at $7.95 . . . . _____

_____ Copies of *Feasting Naturally With Our Friends* at $7.95 . . . . _____

_____ Sets of *Feasting Naturally* Collection — all three of the above books at $17.95 . . . . _____

_____ Please send me a complimentary copy of the *Feasting Naturally Newsletter* . . . . FREE

_____ Brochure(s) *Converting Your Own Recipes* (Limit **one** per coupon/or per book) . . . . FREE

_____ Brochure(s) *Feasting Naturally on a Budget* . . . . FREE

I am interested in Wholesale Distributorships . . . FREE

Postage and Handling (4 or fewer copies) . . . . . . $.95

TOTAL . . . . . . _____

Name: _____

Address: _____

City: _____ State: _____ Zip: _____

Send check or money order to:

Feasting . . . Naturally
P.O. Box 968
Harrison, Arkansas 72601
501-741-7340

★ All Trade Orders (5 copies or more) $4.80 per copy . . .40% Discount

★ All **Prepaid Trade** orders . . . . FREIGHT FREE

★ We accept phone orders, S.T.O.P. orders, Mastercard and Visa.